Learning Leadership

Building Your Professional Career

Charles L. "Chip" Pickering Ph D

Copyright © 2014 Charles Pickering

All rights reserved.

ISBN: 1496133064
ISBN-13: 978-1496133069

DEDICATION

This book is dedicated to my father, Charles E. Pickering. He was very patient with me as I learned how the world works and established the foundations of leadership for me—integrity, honesty and a great sense of humor.

TABLE OF CONTENTS

Acknowledgments

1 Introduction of the Processes

Overview

2 Person, Profession & Adding Value

3 Person & The Organization

4 Person & Perception

5 Personal 'Brand'

6 The Environment

7 Professional Stages

8 Leadership Skills

Technical Skills

9 Welcome to the Working World

10 Depth vs. Breadth

11 Helping Others & Building Relationships

12 Leadership Skills

Professional Skills

13 Project Management

14 Client Focus

15 Team Focus

16 Work Motivation and Drive

17 Emotional Intelligence

18 Leadership Skills

Management Skills

19 Understanding the Organization

20 Adding Value

21 Leveraging Value

22 Management vs. Leadership Skills

Leadership Skills

23 Critical Thinking & Decision Making

24 Shifting Skills

25 Social Intelligence

26 Role of Executive Coach

27 Leadership Processes

Selected Additional Reading

About the Author

Citations

ACKNOWLEDGMENTS

This book is the roadmap that I never had. I entered the construction industry as a young minted engineer working for my family business and the world that I learned was ad-hoc and spontaneous. We lived off of what we killed at the time, but the world to me was whatever opportunity presented itself at the time.

Later in my life I developed a professional mentor, and I thank Jack Derr for befriending our small company and sharing his life experiences with us. He had billions of dollars in constructed project experience when that was a lot of money, and he shared his important lessons with us with a 'now listen, Laddie….'

I thank those wonderful people that I worked with at our construction and engineering and architectural companies. They have all been very patient with me—allowing me to obtain more education than is healthy for a human to have, and being patient when I throw high level concepts around without properly explaining them.

This book is my gift to those young engineers, architects and other professionals that work with me. Their energy and vision have and are still creating an organization which is much better than I could have created by myself. Thank you.

Finally, thanks to Jan, my wife. This book is several years in the making, and it usually happened during vacations, holidays and other opportunities to get away from the 'grind' and be able to focus. For all those days exploring bookstores and quiet evenings reading and processing, I thank you for your patience.

This book is not about business strategy, but about the course that your career takes, and how to look at your future not from the trenches but from a perspective where you can control it.

1 INTRODUCTION OF THE PROCESSES

It's interesting for me to look back now upon my exit from college into the "cruel world" of business. As an engineer I was given a great training on the technical aspects of the engineering world. I was never prepared, however, to practice these technical skills in the business and organizational world that I was entering. Unfortunately, as I was entering into my career environment and trying to figure out how to be successful in my own profession, I did not have a mentor or others that could help me understand what I was trying to achieve. This meant that I was required to try to figure out what success meant and how to achieve it for myself.

I did not know to attempt to seek others who were facing starting into business like myself, as networking and young leader groups were not available within my area. Along the road I was drawn into professional organizations, but these were organizations which were looking out for the profession from a high level and not how to get in, get established and flourish on an individual level.

This book is intended to help provide a high level view of the professional world, and how you as a young professional or business person would enter, grow and become successful in the business world. The goal of this book is to help you identify and develop skills which will help you become a future business leader. This includes helping you:

1) Map out a path forward for personal success within your field or profession,

2) To provide an overview of the skillsets necessary for the professional and leadership requirements at different points along your career path, and

3) To assist, where possible, in identifying strategies for developing, refining and honing these skillsets in an effective way.

Individual Career Progress

This book is intended to provide focus and guidance at various progressive stages of career or professional development. There are two important aspects which underlie this progress—the first is that all career paths are not the same, and thus the timing of and opportunities within these various paths may be accelerated, decelerated or come out of sequence. That is fine—the underlying themes within this book are still valid, and may be applied when they are appropriate within the individual's professional and project growth cycle.

Secondly, no two individuals are the same. Some will have a strong desire to stay within the technical service delivery area and never venture into project management, client management or organizational management. This may be fine as long as the organizational situation can accommodate this specialization. In this case the higher-level skill sets will allow the professional a better perspective of the organization as a whole and how they can be more effective in this organizational and group context. Other professionals may have a goal of accelerating their growth into the management side, in which case the higher-level skills may be focused upon earlier in the individual's career.

Planning Your Future

We use Project Management strategy to plan our successful projects. How many effective projects have ever been delivered where the goal was not clearly defined and articulated, no project controls were in place to see if we were successfully working toward the goals, nor how to correct for deficiencies in our progress. Certainly we respond to changes and opportunities that present themselves during the course of the project, but we always have a goal that we are interested in achieving and which is worth our time and effort.

Certainly our own career is worth a little planning as well? It is important to sit down and conceptualize your future goals, analyze your developing skills and goals periodically and take corrective action as a response. The appropriate steps in this process would be (at a minimum):

1. Identify and clearly articulate your goal. This could include your personal goals with respect to organizational management, future positions and financial returns. This goal could have some contingency built into it to account for variation in the market during your career lifespan and flexibility as other opportunities present themselves.

a. This goal should include work-life balance and the returns that you are looking for from your work efforts. This goal should be shared with any individual in your life who may have a significant interest in your time and family balance. The old adage that nobody's tombstone reads "He wishes he had spent more time at work." applies here. Work responsibilities can multiply and consume time and effort that could compromise your ability to develop and maintain a successful and happy home life, so a barrier should be erected between work and home and periodically checked and actively managed.
2. Once this goal is clearly communicated, the steps to get there should be defined. I outline a generic plan within this book of the various stages that a professional can go through during their life, but it is only general. Your own plan will allow you to have a vision of where you want to go in more detail, but recognize that it can change over time as new opportunities present themselves. This plan should have a general timeline and specific milestones that you can check your progress against.
   a. Create short-term milestones which will allow you to measure your progress. The more detailed you can

get with your plan the better you will be able to measure your progress. These milestones can be the achievement of a professional degree or certification, passing a class or simply studying for 5 hours a week toward a professional exam. We are more willing to work toward a specifically identified and objective goal than a subjective and fuzzy goal.

    b. This plan should have a contingency plan as well. When opportunities present themselves it is important to weigh them against your identified goals. This will allow you to keep your focus on the goal and maintain your performance toward the goal.

3. Begin working toward these goals. If you have done a good job planning the specific skills, competencies and career progress stages you can begin breaking these down and working toward them. Your periodic progress checks toward your milestones will let you know if you are making adequate progress toward your goals.

    a. Here is where mentorship and good feedback is important. Because we all have a flawed perspective about our skills and capabilities, we cannot clearly measure our abilities. Our career progress toward our milestones will provide a high-level

guideline as to how the organization values our efforts, but it also has market-driven and competitive components. A mentor or coach can collect information and help you identify your strengths and help you develop those aspects which are not as strong.
4. Monitoring your performance should drive additional improvements. In a changing world, people that are not working on goals, continuing education and self-improvement are going to be overtaken by their peers.
5. Finally, keep updating your goals. The goals that you had when you were 20 are likely not going to be still driving you when you are in your 50s. The world has also changed in these years since, opportunities have come up that were not anticipated, and your own desires and needs may have shifted. It is important to keep your goals in line with your shifting values and priorities in your life. This can also affect your evolving implementation plan as well. Remember—the plan is not the goal, but its primary value is to identify the immediate next steps and provide a direction for individual improvement.

Leadership

The following are the basic strategies for adopting leadership skills which can be developed at various points in your career development:

1. It all begins through observation. Begin developing the critical thinking skills and perception to be able to identify influence tactics and leadership behaviors that you see being exercised within your organizations (including work and volunteer organizations). How are effective (and ineffective) leaders behaving? How do they communicate with others? Are they effective planners? Do they utilize people's time efficiently and respectfully and are they good communicators? It is through these observations that you can identify behaviors that you like and don't like in others, and these behaviors will begin to mold your perspectives on leadership and organizational efficiency.
    a. Understand the communication and behavior patterns and preferences that other individuals within your peer group have. How can you adapt your communication and behaviors to allow you to adjust to the other individuals in a way that is effective for them?
    b. The organizations have preferred communication patters within them as well. How can you be effective in your communication within and outside the organization and allow yourself to have the most influence with your clients and peers.

2. Learn the basic leadership guidelines. There are general attributes and behaviors that have been associated with leadership—honesty, respect, and having an upstanding character among them. It is important to have these characteristics embedded in your value systems, behaviors and perspectives of others so that they show through genuinely in your dealings with others. How do people respond to the way they are approached by other managers & leaders?
3. Read the appropriate sections of the book which describe the behaviors and perspectives which will allow you to be the most effective at your current career stage. Look ahead and identify the skill sets that you will want to begin to develop for your next career stage and begin to develop these skills. Awareness of these competencies as you look forward will allow you to begin to lay the foundation for these perspectives and behaviors that you will need to rely on in the future. If you are not honest, genuine and empathetic with your peers and subordinates early in your career they will not respect you and trust you in the future.
    a. These skills and perspectives need to be internalized and developed both at the conscious level (adapting social interactions to the needs and preferences of others) and a subconscious level (your feelings and beliefs about the people you

work with—your emotional connection and empathy).
4. Begin to practice these skills and get feedback. How do people respond to you when you approach and interface with them in different ways?
    a. Seek opportunities to stretch yourself. Offer to prepare presentations or reports for others, make presentations to groups of people when possible to develop group communication skills. These will become vital to you when you get a chance to communicate with larger groups.
5. Finally, you will find your own personal style. You will develop your own approaches, favorite techniques and thoughts about others that will resonate with people that are interested in working with you.
    a. These approaches will need to be adaptive to your approach to different individuals.
    b. Leadership approaches and behaviors are also dependent upon the situation. You will need to be able to understand the relationships between the leader-follow dynamic and the various situations that you will be in.

Feedback and Mentoring

It is important to discuss the role of feedback early on in any conversation about professional development. The high-level skill sets that I indicate are important are general in nature. In your own organization's business and in the business environment your supervisor, clients and/or your peers, they may desire or need different behaviors and skills exhibited or others enhanced or downplayed. You will not know what these specific skill sets are without obtaining feedback. The normal feedback process in the business context is known as the annual "performance review", and proves a minimal or poor feedback channel for a future leader's improvement. A proactive individual will seek out and find a way to bring this feedback back in a much more frequent manner (and a Learning Organization will have processes which encourage more frequent and higher quality communication). All new professionals should find a way to obtain "informal" feedback from knowledgeable sources and perhaps assistance in honing their skill sets accordingly.

The way that performance evaluations are implemented (and especially if performed once a year) they are often difficult for both parties and can trigger negative responses from developing professionals. Our ego helps us construct perspectives about our behaviors and the effectiveness of our performance. Because our actual performance as seen by others is often at odds with our held perspectives it causes us tension, frustration and perhaps disappointment. The further along we are in our professional growth sequence the more embedded our ego-related perspectives (and related emotional bonds) can be. One way to properly interpret and internalize this feedback is to consider that the feedback indicates the desired behaviors of the supervisor and/or the management team would like to see, and this feedback *is* subjective. The individual has the opportunity to accept or adapt to the feedback or to take other action as they deem appropriate. Without high-quality, honest feedback, however, the individual does not have the best information for making informed decisions or evaluating their future actions and behaviors.

Organization of this Book

The organization of this book is progressive and is intended to follow the career path of an individual through their professional career. Section 1 comprises the Overview Section, which begins by analyzing the "professional" and career context and the individual's relationship with business organizations. It provides a lens to look at the context of work in a career or profession. It also provides a perspective of the business organization, and how the individual can see him/herself in this interplay. We will introduce the concept of "adding value" from an organizational and individual perspective. This section looks at the environment and how their own situation may change with environmental change (both internal and external to the organization). Finally, an overall career path is introduced which identifies the phases of career progression.

Section 2 introduces the professional's initial stage of development in the context of the development of their Technical Skills. This section builds the case that the professional's initial stage of career development should focus on the development and mastery of their technical skills, progressively developing their skills and automating the technical delivery process. The skills that are important to be developed during this initial phase of the individual's career involve individual performance, group dynamics, self-control and developing a "big picture" perspective.

Section 3 discusses the professional's transition into the project and client management role, including refining their Professional Skills and becoming comfortable managing the client—organization relationships and the delivery of professional services. The skills that are important will be the ability to see the whole project, multi-tasking, good communication skills, teambuilding, refining self-control and moving into developing various personal attributes generally classified as emotional intelligence.

Section 4 provides an introduction to business management processes and skills that will be important understanding the organization as a business, and situating the business in the modern world. Within this section we will not be focusing on the professional's skills and abilities as much as we will be providing the basic operations of management in a professional service context. This section will also help provide the background for understanding the organization as a whole and the other aspects of an organization which are important to the organization's success. This background will be important to the professional's final step.

Section 5 gives the skills and capabilities which are important for leading an organization. Higher level processes are discussed in this area, which build upon the management understandings to allow the leader to organize, motivate and focus employees and others toward the organization's goals. These processes include those generally considered leadership processes, the development of critical thinking skills, and social intelligence. These skill sets are necessary for success at a high level, but are also extremely subjective and difficult to bring about individually. For this reason I introduce the concept of an executive coach—someone that can continue to sharpen and "polish" the tool, bringing it to is highest and best value.

There are multiple ways to read and utilize this book. Initially the new professional should focus on the characteristics which will allow them to be successful at their current stage of development. These are the skills which will provide initial success. The proactive and visionary individuals will then begin looking ahead and identifying, developing and honing the skills which will allow them to successful in future tasks when the opportunity to advance presents itself.

Overview

2 PERSON, PROFESSION & ADDING VALUE

In this section we will begin examining the professional and her relationship with the organization (and the organization's environment). Additionally, the concept of value and the professional's ability to add value to the organization is considered.

The new professional graduates from a university with a newly minted diploma and perhaps some experiences in the real world as a result of their previous employment and internship experiences. They contact, interview and negotiate for a position with an organization. When hired, they are assigned a desk, and begin the learning process again. In the new position the employee begins the process of learning the rules and regulations of governing bodies, new software packages, standard processes of the organization and "norms" in the professional environment that they entered. This is a lot of information to digest, internalize and assimilate. It makes sense that this takes some time. The management of the employing organization knows this, and assumes that the "learning curve" will allow for the eventual acquisition of skills through learning and mentoring processes, and the value of the professional to the organization will increase over time. The rate at which the individual acquires these appropriate skills, and the value of the skills to the organization, will dictate the rate at which the professional's salary can increase. This is also related to the rates that charge for the professional's services to their clients.

The Professional Relationship

It is interesting how we, in a Capitalistic society, have socially created the employer-employee relationship. At a purely theoretical level, in an employment relationship the employee provides or 'leases' a certain amount of their time, skills and energy to the organization in exchange for a wage or salary and other benefits. The value of the individual's time to the organization is proportional to the knowledge, skill level, abilities and motivation that they bring to the relationship. The value of these skills is proportional to the need of the organization for these skills and abilities.

Thus to increase the value of their time, the individual is motivated to increase the skills, knowledge and/or competencies that they can bring to the employer, with the assumption that these skills will be considered valuable to the organization. At the technical level, the organization tends to value skills which increase the production or delivery of services (either internal to the organization or externally). By increasing their production the individual can increase their 'rents', or what they receive in exchange for their time and efforts. Additionally, the value of these services to the client can be enhanced through the building of effective relationships with the client.

There are a couple of unique aspects of professional practice in conjunction with their attendant employment relationships. The first is the recognition that the professional in a regulated profession completes their professional development process individually with the state regulation board. Through training, testing, certification and continuing education, the *individual* is the one that obtains and maintains their professional registration, certifying their competency to practice in their profession. There may be other barriers restricting the employment of professionals, but for all intents and purposes they are able to take their skills (including their professional licenses) to other organizations or practice individually. The employment organization should thus be interested in taking care of the professionals that it wants to have an ongoing relationship with. This means that the organization has an implied goal of creating opportunities for growth for professionals within the organization.

A second aspect of the professional employee, which is worth mentioning, is that they may hold a higher allegiance to their profession than to the organization. One definition cites that the professional 'supplies objective counsel and service to others, for a direct or definite compensation, wholly apart from expectation of other business gain'[i]. Some professions reinforce this with ethical codes and pledges, in one form or another, to put the 'public welfare ahead of personal gain'. As we see the professional becoming a part of the management of the organization, or delivering projects or services for profit, the individual's and the organization's goals of profitability it can provide a tension for the professional employee.

Organizational Value Delivery Process

At this point it would be helpful to explore the value process. Organizations provide value by taking the inputs of materials, labor and other specialized knowledge and providing an output—a product or service which can be sold for a value higher than the sum of the unit cost of the inputs—adding value. These services or products are valued by the clients as they allow them to fulfill the goals of the purchasing organization. The value to the purchasing organization is related to the ability of proportionate value they can get from the service or the amount of cost that they can avoid.

In most professional (and often in service-related industries) there is a subjective aspect to the service delivery. The baseline for service cost is often established by competition in the environment, but higher value professional products and services are based upon established relationships. Additionally, high value ongoing business relationships are built upon knowledge and experiences that both organizations have mutually developed and learned from. This allows for deeper relationships as time goes on, and the ability of the service provider to refine and improve their delivery process for a target client.

Businesses seek to provide high-value services and to provide services to clients who will appreciate the value that they bring. Organizations should continually evaluate their clients in order to determine which clients appreciate the value that they provide and which do not. Clients which do not appreciate the value of the products and services provided should be prioritized at a lower level than those that do.

Individual Value Delivery

In a similar way, as employees enter the workforce and begin to building their competencies, it is helpful to conceptualize the way they do, and can, offer value to the organization. In a similar way to the organization seeking value in their environment, individuals provide value to the organization. This value follows very similar valuation processes—the capabilities that the individual brings to the organization allow the organization to provide values into the environment. The organization is compelled to acquire high-value employees which provide good services into its market and leverage higher returns for the organization.

Thus as the individual grows e should be scanning the organization and the organization's environment to identify which high-value skills and competencies to develop. The higher the value of the skills developed, the higher the value the individual has to the organization (or to other organizations). As an individual goes through their technical growth years they are acquiring skills that may or may not be valued in the organization's future. If the organization is proactive they may be considering future skills in their training and work encouragement, but usually the organization is using the individual's skills to meet current needs. If these opportunities change over time it may be prudent for the individual to seek skills which will be relevant (and high value) in the future market.

This conversation goes back to the professional conversation—that ultimately you are responsible for targeting your continuous learning on high-value opportunities in the future. I like the quote by Wayne Gretske, a famous hockey player who, when he was asked how he always managed to be in the right place at the right time, remarked 'A great hockey player plays where the puck is going to be', not where it is. In a similar way, the professional should be scanning the environment, anticipating what the needs of the organization (and the organization's market or environment) will be in the future, and positioning themselves to be able to take provide these high-value opportunities.

In the organizational management context, organizational development and organizational learning borrow from the concept that the organization should be continually scanning the environment, looking for new technologies and changes which will shift the way that services and products are delivered and the relative value of these products over time. Organizations gather, sort and respond to information (input) from the environment and implement changes and adaptive responses to the environment based upon their evaluation of this information.

In a similar way, individuals need to actively manage their own growth and training. Obviously, skills that are important to the organization and what it sells into its market should be considered a high priority. However, just as an organization scans its environment to look for future opportunities, I would encourage young professionals to consider their own efforts in continual learning and growth as an investment in their own future, and invest these efforts wisely.

3 PERSON & THE ORGANIZATION

In this section we will explore the relationship between the person and the organization. We will analyze this situation in the context of a social contract and practical capitalistic relationship.

Organizations provide the means to fulfill the needs (and wants) that other individuals and organizations have. The organization receives income from these other sources in order to sustain itself. The organization needs people (employees) and perhaps other organizations (subcontractors and sub-consultants) in order to provide a complete product or service to these customers or clients. Organizations purchase tools, rent facilities and purchase the raw materials in order to provide these products or services.

It is often helpful to keep an objective perspective on this organization we consider our business. We can conceptualize the organization as a living, breathing organism—one which is focused on bringing in and servicing high value clients. As with any organism, it is interested in surviving (and, if it can, thriving), by providing good services which can maximize its income. An appropriate consideration for the organization, is acquiring, training and utilizing the best resources that it can afford in order to provide the best goods and services to its market. With these high value returns it can therefore provide profits to its owners and additional returns to its principles.

It helps to conceptualize the business as an organization with goals, and which needs high quality employees to provide high-value services to its clients. This concept will help to begin to consider the employee-employer relationship.

The Employment Relationship

Individuals (employees) seek out organizations which will help them meet their personal goals and will give them opportunities to grow and develop professionally and personally. They also seek organizations with corporate cultures and value systems that are aligned with their own. Upon being hired, the new employee begins to experience the organization, and the organization begins an evaluation of the new employee. The employee encounters and experiences the organization's culture upon the orientation and initial employment.

At the entry level (and often for new employees with experience) the compensation package is usually fixed in conjunction with a range or norm within the industry, adjusted for local living costs, special skills, capabilities and experiences which are valued by the organization and balanced by the local need for these particular competencies. The employer evaluates the skills and capabilities of the employee, and is compelled to increase the compensation as the employee develops additional skills and experience that are valuable to the employer.

At the technical level, ultimately the returns that the professional can get in exchange for their time is often set by the client. In a direct consulting or service relationship the industry has a general pre-set value established for the hourly services of a professional with a given amount of experience. This can vary depending upon many different situations including relationships among the provider-client organizations and the business environment at the time. Because these services, in a mature market, are fungible, the market would have a relatively precise range for the value of these services. Generally, this puts the professional into a compensation range based upon their skills, competencies and knowledge.

Thus, during the initial stages of an individual's development, when the organization is selling the professional's **technical skills** in the local market, the way for an individual to advance their salary and position within the organization is to develop new and higher value skills and knowledge *that is valuable to the organization & the organization's customers*.

As the professional develops her skills (and perhaps achieves registration or professional certification) she will have advanced beyond simply providing technical services, and may have begun to provide other higher-value processes. Because these **professional services** often provide more value by aggregating different technical professions for the delivery of a project or service, it provides a higher value to the organization, and allows an opportunity for growth within the organization.

In many areas this process falls under the general concept of **project management**. In project management, the manager works with the client to identify a project scope (what needs to be done), a budget and timeframe for the implementation, and assures the project's delivery to the client—the final product or service. Generally, the client's perception of the quality of the services is a function of 1) the value of the final product or service, and 2) the experience that the client and the organization had in fulfilling this product. In this light, it is clear that the delivery of the product and the delivery experience are important to the organization, and the person that is coordinating the production and delivery of the product and the client's experience in the process is very important to the organization. Delivering projects successfully allows the opportunity for financial and personal growth within the organization.

Once an employee becomes comfortable in their project management role, providing completed projects to the client, they may be asked to provide additional **management responsibilities** within the organization. When and how this may happen is a function of the organization's size, management structure and other factors. Presuming that it is right for the individual and the organization, the professional's movement into management usually requires additional skills and knowledge that they would not necessarily acquire during their technical or professional (project management) development. This is why Executive MBA programs are so popular—at the time the professional has acquired the knowledge of the industry and is ready to begin guiding and managing the organization they have a resource to begin to acquire the knowledge required to properly assume additional responsibilities, manage other employees and provide direction to the organization.

Finally, a few of the professionals demonstrate the appropriate capabilities to provide high-level management and **organizational leadership**. Often these positions include compensation incentives tied to organizational performance and/or stock ownership within the organization. Again, the quantity and skills required for these leadership positions varies significantly between organizations and their attendant cultures, but all organizations need good leadership at all levels.

The goal of this book is three fold. The first is to identify the skills and competencies that will be important to the growing professional at their current level of development and organizational responsibilities. Secondly it also can give the individual an opportunity to "look ahead" and begin to identify leadership skills and capabilities which will be important as they grow into future positions and opportunities. Finally, and most importantly, because leadership skills can be learned, the professional will be able to identify, acquire and practice skills that they will eventually need and put themselves in positions to practice the development of these leadership competencies.

4 PERSON & PERCEPTION

One of the interesting things about human beings, as advanced as we are (or perceive ourselves to be), is that we can only see the world through our limited perception. This has some very important implications for us, which we will explore in the following sections.

Information Gathering and Processing
The first of these implications is that the that the world, as extremely vast and complicated as it is, in order to be real to us, must be perceived and interpreted through our senses. These senses are the ways that 'data' gets introduced into our minds for us to analyze, organize and interpret. (As a matter of fact, there is an interesting argument in metaphysics about whether or not there is a reality or whether we are just having some data introduced to us that we are interpreting as reality. Another is whether we are all experiencing the same stimuli and interpreting it the same way—for example, is my concept of blue the same as yours?)

From the time we were young we have been gathering data, organizing it, and sorting this data into recognizable patterns. Based upon this concept, everything that you 'know' has come to you as data through your senses, and been sorted and organized by you (or for you). Thus your thought processes, perspectives and belief systems are provided through development, training and social programming. From 'right and wrong' to social positions and values—all of these perspectives have been created through the processing of data from the world and other people's assistance in interpretation of that data.

Heuristics

One of the important aspects of our brains is that we are good at spotting patterns. We have developed as a species looking for patterns and especially at identifying and responding to patterns that are threatening to us. As we grow up we develop patterns which we use to sort information and classify information, behavior, 'right or wrong', 'good or bad', beauty, and much more. These 'rules' are called heuristics, and we use them to interpret information that we are receiving on a continual basis—not even being aware of the evaluations that are being made. These heuristics have a foundation on our value systems and allow us to be able sort and interpret all manner of input which we receive.

Some of these rules may not be correct, however. Because they are built through education and social interaction, the concept of right or wrong can be as diverse as our individual learning experiences (take for example the concept of abortion, and you will find opinions clear across the spectrum based upon the data and social construction of the individual norms present). Thus the complex heuristic processes that we all hold are individual to ourselves and are based upon our upbringing, experiences and cultural norms. In fact, different cultures are often evaluated based upon the collective groups of norms that they hold.

Biases

Humans have a tenancy to make decisions and evaluate information incorrectly based upon built-in tendencies and processes called biases. Interestingly, we humans have an innate ability to over-value our contribution to a group goal and to generally think that we perform better than other people believe that we do. This is an individual bias which is a significant contributor to your ego. Because of the way that we receive information from the environment and interpret it through our biased perspectives, we tend to over-estimate our contribution to a goal and under-estimate the contributions of others that participated.

This bias, in our later career, allows successful managers and leaders to over-estimate their own contribution and neglect to reward those individuals who have performed well. This is a major mental fallacy which can trip up a bright future, and it is built into our psyche.

As a matter of fact, this is one reason why it is difficult for some people to receive criticism—especially criticism which contrasts with their personal perspectives about their performance. Many individuals who cannot accept constructive criticism will hit a ceiling in their career. Unless people can develop the capacity to look objectively at themselves and modify the behaviors and approaches that do not work with other people, they will never advance to their full potential.

Unfortunately, a person's self-image, especially if they associate much of their sense of self-worth with their professional performance, is connected to deep-seeded emotional tags. People spend a lot of their waking hours at work, and connect a large portion of their sense of self to their career, profession and personal competencies. When these beliefs and images are challenged by data to the contrary, the emotional tags associated with this information can be a significant driver in the interpretation (or rejection) of that information. Many people do not want to hear, and are generally not open to, constructive criticism. Because it makes people uncomfortable, they don't want to give criticism either. However if good information is not offered and positively received, how can we improve?

Humility
Humility is the long-recognized attribute that allows a person to consciously avoid over-emphasizing their own importance. This is a healthy attribute or perspective to cultivate early in a professional's career because it allows us to be open to other people's opinions and personal improvements. Additionally, other people are much more receptive and friendly towards someone who is humble, which creates a good environment for working together going forward. The seeds that are planted early in a professional's career will be harvested later in their career. Many people look toward the leader from the perspective of how he/she behaved when they were 'in the trenches'

and whether they respect and appreciate the contributions of others. These are all appropriate responses from people with humility.

Information Overload (Cognitive Scope Limitation)
Think about all of the sources of information that would be available to a person at any given time. Hundred channels on the TV, multiple available newspapers, magazines, and virtually unlimited amounts of information on the internet, email, books at the library and online. There is much more information available to a person than they could possibly process at any given time. Even walking down the street on a peaceful evening—there is much more information available than could ever be processed and stored.

To deal with this, humans have developed elaborate processes for sorting information. What a person allows into their life and pays attention to makes up the data set that they use to make decisions. These decisions are then based upon limited information and interpreted based upon the person's *schema* (worldview or understanding of how the world is or should be). It is for this reason that new disruptive technologies are created not within the large corporations that command the existing technologies but from people on the outside with a new perspective (Stephen Jobs studied art and marketing).

The sources that we gather information from pre-sort this information to us, and provide much of the interpretation for this information as well. We cannot get away from other people collecting, sorting and interpreting information to us. Our responsibility, then, is to balance these information channels so that we get a spectrum of information from which to make decisions.

Decision Making

In a similar way that biases affect our self-perception and heuristics mold our interpretation of information, humans have (sometimes inefficient) processes developed for decision-making. These standard processes then often lead us to incorrect decisions. An abbreviated list of these processes which may lead us to make mistakes in our decision-making processes include:

- Loss aversion—people do not want to lose what they have more than they are interested in gaining more. Often the way a decision is posed biases us toward a particular course of action or decision.
- Recency—people have a tendency put a higher weight on information which was provided more recently.
- Contrast—the way options are presented can bias people's ability to compare options
- Scarcity—related to loss aversion, if people feel that something is scarce or may not be available in the future they will be biased toward action to protect it.

Recognizing that this is a partial list, it is not appropriate at this time to list all of the biases associated with decision making. Future sections of this book, however, will introduce activities and processes which will help avoid some of these critical decision-making biases.

Much of the information presented in this section helps you as a professional, moving through your upward career path, to have some background information into how self-perception and heuristics affect your processing and decision making. In later chapters, as concepts are introduced concerning behaviors and processes which should be incorporated into your activities and perspectives, these concepts will be the foundations for these processes.

5 PERSONAL 'BRAND'

At its lowest level, the concept of a 'brand' is the association that people make between the organization and the products and services that they provide. Marketing tells us that there is much more to a brand. Think about the premium brands that you are familiar with—Rolex, BMW, Cartier, Mercedes-Benz, Armani as examples. These names invoke more than just the products that they represent; they invoke stories, relationships, mystique and expectations of the products. These names represent concepts of success and are connected with emotional tags that we have internalized associated with these products. These connections are the results of careful branding processes which you have received and internalized over time.

Organizational Brands
If you own or have owned these products in the past, you may have experienced a sense of superior performance or quality, but you almost certainly experienced a sense of pride while using these products. This is intentional and is a combination of your perceptions of these products and the social cues associated with the product ('the ultimate driving machine'.)

Organizations spend lots of time, effort and resources creating, fine-tuning and maintaining the message of the brand. They spend a lot of time considering the images and messages that are presented and the messages that will be interpreted from them. The images and feelings that are evoked from these brands are important to the value processes that they provide.

Providing Value

As we discussed earlier, businesses generate revenues through a process of taking inputs (raw materials, resources, money) and provide outputs (products or services) which add value. This additional value provides profits, which can be utilized to create new or improve existing products or services or achieve other organizational goals. The branding of the premium brands allows the products to be sold at a higher value, providing more revenues to pursue these organizational goals. Some of this additional profit is spent maintaining the 'brand', the image, emotion and social cues associated with the product you are receiving. Through aggressive marketing, successful organizations spend lots of time and resources identifying, perfecting and defending their brand.

Earlier we learned that individuals provide value in much the same way as organizations do. We have skills and capabilities which allow us to contribute to the organization's goals. The perceived value of the contribution produces rewards and incentives from the organization for our contributions. The higher the value of our contributions as they relate to increasing the value to the client or customer, the higher the rewards that are available to you as the employee.

In a service corporation the customer's experience is directly related to the quality of the services provided by the employee(s). Thus, as the value of the employee's service delivery increases the value of the delivered product increases, mediated by the competitive market. Organizations that expend the effort to build high-value services and an appropriate 'brand' have an opportunity to take advantage of the premium perspectives.

Personal Brand

In a similar way, you have the ability to develop your own personal 'brand'. As I indicated before, one of the things that is most important is the *perceived* value of the employee's contribution toward the organization's goals. Early in your career you should become aware of the image that is projected to both the organization's management and your peers. Your individual brand is a combination of the perspectives of everyone that interacts with you during your working experience, including the way that you personally add value to the organization.

Self-awareness

The first aspect of managing the way others perceive you is developing a sense of self-awareness. This is one of the most difficult but important aspects of your self-improvement, and may eventually help establish the level of success that you will achieve in your business career. At the initial level the concept of self-awareness includes attention to your looks, dress, mannerisms and behaviors. Your behaviors, however, are the outward product of the values, attitudes and belief systems that you hold at your core, and are difficult to describe and isolate because they are ingrained in your "self". The way you behave toward others is a reflection of your perspective of their value, and your true interest in what they are thinking and saying. Because people can tell whether or not you are being genuine, or true to your belief systems, it is important to develop be able to isolate and consider your internal value systems.

At this point take some time and create a list of what you consider your core value systems. What is good and bad, right and wrong, how should people be treated, and what are your goals in life. What would you consider your life having been "successful" if you accomplished? Another way to consider this is to write your own epitaph—what would you have them say about you when you are gone? It is important to develop your core beliefs because you will want to have them firmly planted in your thoughts so that your behaviors and feelings can truly reflect these perspectives.

One of the problems that we human beings have is that we have a hard time objectively looking at ourselves. It is difficult to step out of our perspectives, and out of our world, and analyze how we behave, come across or act toward others. That's why it is important to have someone who will give you frank feedback about your behavior and actions on an ongoing basis. It is difficult to provide criticism to a friend because this feedback questions or challenges so much of who we are.

When we receive feedback (or criticism) it is filtered through our ego, or our sense of self-esteem and self-importance. Most people have an inflated ego at least at some level, and over-value their contributions. If you can, early in your career, begin to control your ego and learn to seek and fully process feedback and constructive criticism. By doing this you will be building a skill that will allow you to adapt your strengths and behaviors as your career advances and you need to be able to learn and exhibit new skills.

Additional Competencies

At the core of your personal brand will be your *character*. What you develop on the outside is a *reputation*, but this is grounded in your character. If you can guard your personal feelings and attitudes, building upon positive virtues and humanistic perspectives, you will have a foundation to be truly kind, gentle and empathetic. These attributes of your character will be what others build their long-term trust and relationships upon— relationships that will serve you well later in life. You don't want to be nice to people because it will help you in the future, you want to be nice to people because it is so innate in your character that you could not think of behaving any differently.

Another important competency is that of *self-regulation.* Are you able to devote yourself to self-advancement and professional growth before recreation? Are you able to deny yourself short-term gratification for longer-term and higher rewards? When you are faced with frustrating situations are you able to step back, allow the frustration to abate, and respond in a controlled and well-managed manner? These are all skills that are important for you to develop early in your career. As you move into project management and organizational management you will be faced with increasingly difficult and frustrating situations. How you respond to these situations is important to both you and the others that are working with you. You will need to be able to make correct decisions and implement them in a cool and comfortable manner despite the tensions of the world around you.

With respect to self-regulation, it is important to recognize that you cannot control many of the situations and problems that the world throws at you—you can only control your response to these situations. It is important early in your professional life to be able to step out of your skin and be able to process the situation without (or at least minimizing) an emotional response. Emotions cloud the ability to think and act clearly and effectively, so this skill is one that you should be working on early in your career.

Finally, people want to work with people that are *reliable, honest* and *friendly*. These character attributes should be foremost in your mind. Without these at your core you will never be a successful leader. You should always be truthful and *avoid gossip*, especially if it is not productive or absolutely necessary. People realize that if you gossip about others you would likely gossip about them under different circumstances. Keep to the facts and present information clearly and honestly, giving other people the benefit of the doubt.

Finally, people want to associate with people that are *passionate* about their work, projects, clients and the people that they work with. Passionate people generate their own energy, and pass it around to the people that they meet. Develop the capacity to generate internal energy and a positive mental attitude and carry it with you.

These skills and competencies have been introduced to allow you to look at yourself from the perspective of a tool—something that works with the organization to provide a product or service. The quality or 'value' of that product or service allows the organization to satisfy its clients and command higher returns for its services. In the same way, you develop your own 'brand', to establish the quality of services that you personally provide and that the organization and that other employees can rely upon and trust.

6 THE ENVIRONMENT

One of the underlying questions in Organizational Theory is why and how we join together with other people in groups.

In this complex world it is very difficult to be able to comprehend all of the specialized systems and relationships necessary to live in the lifestyle that we do. For a simple example, imagine that the only way that we could travel in a car would be that we obtained all of the materials and made it for ourselves. Beyond that, we could only drive it on the pavement that we personally created. This thought process is a bit absurd, but it begins to introduce our independence with each other. If you consider the levels of organizations that we belong to, it begins with our national citizenship, state, community, business organization, church, family and goes on. Some of these groups we have been born into and have not thought much about, and some we have wilfully joined and there are some that we have left over time.

Each of these organizations allow us to be able to take our personal skills and interests and put them together with others to achieve goals that we could not achieve ourselves working independently. If you think about your life, you belong to many groups, all of which provide you some benefit (either tangible or emotional) for which you exchange some part of you (your time, resources, or interest). We are a gregarious species—we seek out and value others which allow us to meet our personal interests and goals.

If we consider our world on a macro (large) level, we belong to our country through our citizenship. Many have not chosen this, but it has been assigned based upon our birth and/or family ties. There are many benefits that we derive from this association—as an example, can you imagine trying to defend your family against an assault from a foreign army by yourself? By being part of a country we can collect taxes and build a defensive army to be able to protect our borders.

On a micro (small) level we also get together with others to achieve our goals. The work organization is a great example of this. As a professional or developed in your career, you are interested in building specialized skills which are valuable in the world and for which you can command a premium price for your time. In order to leverage your skills you may need to get together with others with complementary skills in order to provide a complete package of services to a customer. You will also need to be in an organization which has a marketing and sales component to connect the organization with clients; which has financial resources to purchase the tools and rent the office that you will operate in, and that bills and collects the resources from the client, pays your salary and distributes the withheld taxes, benefits and other programs that the organization offers. In this way a business organization put individuals together with complimentary skill sets for the various tasks that it needs to complete, organizes these into business sectors, solicits work, manages its completion and coordinates delivery and collection and re-distribution of these resources. Imagine doing this for yourself in order to gain the value from your skills within your chosen profession.

Organizations, like individuals, also have a personality. It has a set of "rules" that it goes by as it deals with the individuals—how they behave, are rewarded, have and use various types of power, and deals with its customers (or clients). This personality is usually referred to as the organization's *culture* (or sometimes referred to as its *climate*). This culture is the set of behaviors that underlies how the individuals interact with each other, creates the norms that are the foundations of the interrelationships with other organizations, and sets the expectations for the individual's interactions with the client.

Organization as an Organism

I would like to build upon a concept that I introduced earlier that will help us further conceptualize the organization in its environment. In Organizational Theory we have been taught that it is helpful to conceptualize the business organization as an object, and I find a lot of value of the conception as an organism. Interestingly, the obvious English language root of the words organism and organization are the same. In fact, the organization is defined as an artificial (or social) entity which was created to meet the goals of the individuals that created it. Similar to an organism (and you can play with this metaphor—an animal, machine, human, etc.) the business needs to get resources from the environment (inputs), provides some useful purpose (throughput) and provide a product (output) from which it can obtain a return (money, in this case) which it can use to build itself up and obtain additional resources (inputs). If the environment change and there is no longer a need for the products that it produces (the favorite illustration of this has always been buggy whips upon the advent of the automobile) the business must adapt its process to produce something else that is useful in the new environment or it will cease to exist. It may be able to live off of its stored resources for some period of time, but eventually it will not last long without making a viable and valuable product or service (output).

I am describing these aspects of the organization to provide a foundation for looking at the organization's environment—the world that the organization lives in. Just as there are factors that affect us in our local world, the organization needs to be aware of its environment and adapt to changes in this environment. This usually means scanning and watching the environment, identifying new trends and opportunities, being aware of current markets which may be diminishing, and identifying the needs that its customers have. How well it can identify these needs and opportunities in the environment and create products that fill these needs (especially the high-value needs) will determine how successful the organization is in the long-term.

Environments and Environmental Change

One of the things that are evident in our world is that it is changing at an ever-increasing rate. If you are in your 50s and at the peak of your career you grew up with color TV as a new concept, computers were owned by NASA or the government when you went to school, copiers did not exist, fax machines came about at mid-career, people had CB radios in their cars if they wanted to communicate, and phones had wires connected to them. The world has changed many times over during this period, and the technologies that worked yesterday were discarded or are sitting on a shelf in the basement and available for nostalgic reflection when visited.

How well a business understands the world that it lives in, its "environment", identifies important aspects that are changing, and adapting to this change determines whether it exists or prospers. Effective organizations gather information from its environment, interprets this information, and adapts itself to these changes. As the dinosaurs can attest, if the world changes and your organism cannot adapt to these changes, they die.

Effective organizations that gather, process and collectively interpret information gathered from the environment fall under the category of the Learning Organization. The Learning Organization is constantly gathering information on its clients , the environment, competition and internally from its constituents, processing this information, looking for trends, and instituting changes based upon this information. When the direction of new changes in the environment is not clearly known it often probes the environment to see what may be effective. Experimentation with new techniques, technologies, tools and services are all examples of probing the environment to see what may be effective and to build competencies which may be valuable in the future environment. Organizations which can do this and are successful at anticipating the environmental change and adapting quickly will thrive; those that cannot adapt may survive (or may not).

Depending upon where you are on your career ladder, you may have different roles in this environmental scanning and processing program. If you are early in your career you may have experienced the newest technologies during your education and can share this with the organization. Clearly you have a perspective of what is working or not working on the ground, and can offer this input to the decision makers in the organization. You can also be alert to spotting the trends in the industry and be suggesting courses of action to the management team that can implement training, new technologies and be seeking new skills to be able to adapt the organization's services to the future environment.

If you are at the management level, your ability to gather information from the environment, interpret this information and make effective decisions will determine whether the organization will be adaptive and proactive or reactive.

Organizations that are able to anticipate the future opportunities and position themselves well to take advantage of these opportunities will thrive.

As we discuss an organization's environment we should be aware that internal changes within the organization can drive change just as changing environments and customers will. New management, mergers or acquisitions could come shifting priorities within the organization and drive the need for new skill sets and capabilities.

It is also important to note that environmental change cannot always be anticipated. The best organizations cannot anticipate disruptive technologies or large-scale environmental changes. Just as cell phones revolutionized communication and personal computing, disruptive technologies completely changes the playing field, or 're-shuffles the deck.' Successful organizations have contingency plans, have reserves available for re-direction, and are agile and can respond to these changes. An attribute of these successful organizations is that they can pivot, shift their skills and resources quickly to adapt to the new needs of the environment.

Personal Skills

In the same way that the organization will thrive or survive, the value of your skills in the future will be dependent upon multiple factors. First, each organization has a set of clients with which it has developed ongoing relationships. These organizations have specific needs, and the skill sets which provide solutions to these needs has will be more valuable. Finally, as these clients and environment changes, the organization's needs may change as well.

      Just as the organization is anticipating producing products or providing services which will be highly valued in the future, you should be building your own personal skills and competencies in order to maximize your own personal returns from the exchange transaction with the organization in this anticipated future. As you are anticipating the organization's changes in the future, building your own personal competencies to help the organization provide these services will maximize your personal opportunities. Additionally, career path development provides opportunities for higher value contributions to the organization's goals.

      Also note that you need to have contingency planning available as well, to be open to change and have the ability to acquire new skills or to adapt to changing environments to help the organization adapt to environmental change and new opportunities.

      In the following sections we will begin to consider your progress through your career path and how that path provides stages for analysis of your contribution to the organization at these various points.

7 PROFESSIONAL STAGES

The concept around this book is that there is a career development path and discernable stages that many professional careers follow, and that during these various points on this career path there are opportunities to develop and practice unique and different leadership skills and competencies. In the following sections we will examine a prototypical career path from the individual's entry into the organization to their ultimate potential position in organizational leadership. These career stages include the development of technical competencies, professional skill development, acquisition and use of management skills, and finally organizational leadership. In the following sections I will provide an initial development of these stages. Each of these stages will be further developed in future chapters in this book.

Technical Skills. Upon completion of their initial career-based educational program the individual joins an organization and begins to develop and practice their professional skills in the context of the legal, regulatory and professional environment. They begin learning about the internal processes of the business, the culture, and how their profession is practiced in that particular environment. During this period the young professional acquires technical skills and increases efficiency, and often acquires a technical or professional certification or registration.

Professional Skills. As the individual becomes competent with their technical skills they will begin to get the opportunity to work with the client, managing the client relationship and/or project delivery. This requires new skill sets, including Project Management, human relationship management skills and higher-levels of organizational and conceptual capacity.

Management Skills. The next step that many successful professionals often take will include some levels of management responsibility. This could include accounting oversight, group management, technical group leader, production responsibilities, procurement or some other responsibilities outside of their technical field. It is good if these responsibilities happen to follow the individual's interests and skills. This is often the time when an executive MBA class or some other formal management training may be introduced.

Organizational Leadership. A few of the top managers will be asked to provide leadership to the organization. The individuals that are positioned for this opportunity will have the skills to able to think strategically and critically, communicate well, make effective decisions and have the appropriate leadership skills to influence and motivate the employees. These skills are available to many professions as they develop, and through the course of this book we will not only identify these skills but look for opportunities to develop them so that you are prepared when opportunity knocks.

8 LEADERSHIP SKILLS

Through the progress of this book I have two goals. First, I will be identifying the skills and competencies that will allow you to be successful at various stages of your career development. Additionally I am looking for opportunities to introduce, develop and nurture your leadership skills so that when you have the opportunity to advance in your career we will be prepared and well positioned for these new opportunities.

One of significant aspects of your personal development will be to lay the foundations of leadership early in your career. First of all, if you were not cooperative, friendly and a good follower earlier in your career people will be hesitant to feel that you are worthy of working with and following in the future. Second, learning and exercising leadership competencies in the future will allow you to be successful in your current career position as well as positioning for future leadership opportunities.

Defining Leadership

Let's initially establish an understanding of the concept of leadership and how that will relate to our current handling of these concepts and the development of personal skills in alignment with organizational leadership. I should warn you that there are many definitions of leadership, and these definitions all drive or are related to a particular focus on leadership skills, competencies and situations. I personally like the concept of leadership as the *motivational interaction between several individuals or groups of individuals in a particular situation*. Through this definition the goal of leadership is to achieve the outcome or goal that the leader has in mind, and requires the appropriate interaction of the leader's behaviors, receptiveness of those who would be led (referred to as the *followers*) in a particular situation (the *environment*, or sometimes the *context* if relating to a particular situation). From an organizational leadership standpoint, the leader is usually someone in a position of power who is motivating people toward the achievement of an organizational goal.

This is usually considered to be beyond the responsibilities of the *manager*, who is responsible for the day-to-day activities of the employees in the achievement of their work outcomes. The manager is directing the activities of the organization, making sure that everything is completed in the appropriate time, and balancing the organization's resources to achieve these outcomes. Once you reach the top level of management, however, you will have other responsibilities—like organizational direction and strategy, motivating and retaining the organization's key employees, and developing deep and lasting relationships with the organization's key clients. Being effective in these areas require leaders to be effective in areas beyond simply managing the organization's processes.

Leadership through Career Stages

As we read this book and progress through the career stages, we will identify the appropriate leadership skills and personal attributes that contribute to success at these various points in the career path.

Initially as we are developing our technical skills we will focus on becoming a good corporate citizen, being reliable, friendly and establish fundamental core value systems which will allow you to make friends and establish credibility, which will be important later in your career. You will need to learn to participate in groups and be counted on to deliver your portion of projects and increase your own technical skills and efficiency. You will want to use this time to develop your personal competencies and interpersonal skills. Finally, you may begin the process of critical thinking—looking at the larger picture, how projects, teams and organizations come together to deliver successful (and unsuccessful) projects and learn from opportunities and problems. This will allow you to have the skill sets to successfully transition into the professional phase of your career.

In the professional phase you will need to have developed (or develop) an understanding of project and organizational production processes. You will become responsible for managing groups of people in order to achieve project outcomes and/or provide client services. You will certainly be leveraging your ability to see the big picture, and understand not only your technical skills but those of the other team members. Your time will be spent understanding the client's expectations, clearly articulating the project requirement steps and outcomes, educating the client and the team members about the detailed project outcomes, measuring and controlling your group's progress toward the goal and communicating the status among all of the relevant stakeholders. You will do this through the management of teams and work groups, either internal to the organization or external. The value system that you developed for yourself and your previous history of technical project delivery will in part determine your success in effectively leading individuals toward the project (or client) goals.

  At some appropriate time in your career if you have mastered the professional aspect of the business you may be asked to assume some management responsibilities. This is often a major shift in skill sets—from managing small group performance to complete project or production goals to understanding organizations, how the operate and integrate, and manage portions of the organization. Understanding the special requirements of a business operation (or group or division) is often a different set of knowledge bases and competencies which are related to, but unique from, their professional skills. Many of the leadership processes are similar between the professional and management roles—those of interpersonal relationships, communication undergirded by personal integrity. Unique competencies may be organized around the specific management responsibilities required. Through your management role you will get the opportunity to see the larger picture of the organization, its deficiencies, strengths, and relationship with its environment. How well you internalize and manage these new skills, as well as your emotional, social and professional development, will determine if you plateau at this level or move on to the top organizational management or leadership.

A few individuals are given the opportunity to move into organizational leadership—the ability to understand the requirements of the organization and integrate these effectively with the customers and environment. People that are selected for, and successful in, organizational leadership have a larger perspective, cultivate a strategic mindset, understand the individual needs and general dynamics within the organization, can conceptualize environmental change and the organization's need for adaptation, and can personally adapt and motivate an organization and its members. These individuals have acquired and honed a group of skill-sets which allow them to be present with, read and motivate employees, understand and satisfy clients, and read the organization's market and adapt the organization to the changing needs of the organization's environment. Fortunately, many of the skills and competencies that you need to be successful in this role can be identified early, learned, honed and perfected so that when opportunities open up you are prepared for them.

Let's begin by looking at the new entrant to the organization, and how they can begin to enter, interpret and understand the organization around them and begin to develop their technical and social skills.

Technical Skills

9 WELCOME TO THE WORKING WORLD

Students and young professionals can have an extreme variation of experiences, including personal, educational and vocational, prior to graduating from a university, college or school and staging their working career. They may have had previous experiences working in other career fields, volunteering in non-profit organizations and/or indenturing or apprenticing in trades prior to this career opportunity.

The initial work experience can also be varied. Experienced individuals could enter into an advanced position or a hybrid position with some management responsibilities. The size of the organization can also dictate whether the new entrant may have a narrow discipline-related focus or may be assigned multiple roles to fill in a day.

Mentor

Obviously I am not going to nail everyone's experience or always speak directly to your own skill sets, needs and support that you might need. There are people within the organization or within your circle of friends, however that can. I would encourage you early on to begin to look around and identify leaders that you admire within or parallel with the organization that you could begin to meet with just to understand the professional terrain and, hopefully, to help you interpret some of this information and give you specific advice about how you might personally build your own competencies.

These mentors can provide a rich interpretation of your initial work experiences and introduce you to successful strategies for success. They can also taint and sour your initial experiences, providing negative interpretations of the organization or fixating on aspects of the organization which have been interpreted as problematic to them. Because your frames for reality and thus your interpretation of data are socially constructed, obtaining the proper perspective will determine whether you will be motivated to grow and be successful or stagnate and be bitter throughout your career.

It is important to realize, also, that the initial organization that you enter may or may not be the environment that you finally choose to mature and grow in. There are certainly things that you can learn from this initial organization—how to become personally competent and effectively work with others. If you choose to move to another organization later you can take the rich experiences with you and also the knowledge of what has worked well in the previous organizations, and what may not have.

Also, keep in mind that in each community, high-performing professionals are limited and are not stagnant. The relationships that you develop early on in your career can turn around and reap rewards for you in the future. I have worked for many professionals that are successful in other organizations and which worked for our firm at one time. It has allowed me to develop personal relationships with them which provide opportunities for deep relationships going forward. It's a small world!

Technical or Professional Competence

All industries or professions have their own tests, metrics or requirements for professional certification. Be it a bar exam, CPA, professional engineer certification or other form of certification, the competency and experience necessary to achieve your professional certification should be your initial goal. This indicates to the world that you have met the minimum competencies for practice in the industry or have mastered the general body of knowledge in the technical area in which you are practicing. Often there are barriers to practice or work in your field without completing the formal certification requirements—this is a minimum requirement and you should expend a good bit of your effort, as appropriate, in obtaining the minimum competency certification in your area.

Beyond that, and especially in the technical and scientific disciplines, changes are happening at a blinding speed. You should have a membership in a professional or technical society in your discipline so that you can read up on and be aware of new technologies, tools, software and methodologies in your industry and in the industries of your customers. These are also excellent locations for professional networking opportunities where you can meet with others and share intimate conversations in a casual environment.

    What are the magazines that your customer reads, what groups do they participate in, and where do they get their information. If you can determine where your customer's industry is going and what the needs that they will have that your organization can satisfy you will have a good leg up on your organization's competition. (Of course, in order for your organization to be able to use this information effectively and position itself to satisfy those future needs, it will have to have an effective information gathering, interpretation and response mechanism to take your feedback and convert it to opportunities.)

    Another way to enhance your value to your organization and to determine industry trends and leaders is through professional networking. If you can put yourself among other like-minded professionals (and especially your clients or others that work with them) and share information you will be able to determine what the best practices are that are being utilized, where the opportunities will be, and how you can best position yourself and your organization to take advantage of these industry trends. This information gathering, interpretation, and network creation will help you throughout your career development.

    If there is no formal networking opportunities among your peers and employers, create one. One of the high-value opportunities for professional and certified technical persons is the requirement for continuing professional development. As fast as the industry changes and new products, methods and processes are being developed, incorporate education in the value-added process that your clients get from you. The real value here, though, is providing quality information that is valid for their needs. There is a lot of information floating around, and you don't want to be providing more noise. Make sure that the training is worth the time that they would be investing.

Time is a Valuable Commodity
From the moment that you start with an organization, begin to study time. There are classes, organizational tools and mental processes that will help you become effective in allocating and using your time. I would suggest you develop a plan and continually update the way that you are allocating time. Because the organization that you work for is likely paying you for your time (in additional to your skills, which become increasingly valuable) there are two ways that the organization can benefit incrementally more from your time. The first is, obviously, that you become more efficient at what you do. If the organization is selling your output by the project they will increase their profitability from your increased output. If the organization is selling your time on an hourly basis your customers will become increasingly pleased with your performance and appreciate the added value.

The second opportunity for leveraging your skills is when you are able to bring in other subordinates and supervise them to deliver additional production for the unit cost. In either case you are adding value to the organization on a task level and they will have an opportunity to increase the compensation for you at some point.

In either case, your time—whether it is being paid for by the organization during business hours or in your leisure, is valuable to you. If you are going to invest time and resources into learning new skills or reading professional literature, allocate that time like you would time at work. If you are not going to get the same value out of your 'investment' in an activity, you may reconsider participating.

Continuous Learning

Especially in the rapidly changing world that we live in, knowledge is king! In the career cycle where technical growth and development is important, take advantage of any educational experience that you can participate in. If you stop and think about it, any *valuable* knowledge and skills that you can learn at this point in your career you can leverage for additional value throughout your career cycle. Just like retirement investment early, education at the beginning of the career cycle will reap compounded rewards.

Aggressively seeking and participating in continuous learning opportunities is a great habit to get into early in your career. Just like any habit, once you establish it in your life it becomes a part of you and your behavior patterns. How much TV do you watch in a week? How much gaming or internet surfing do you participate in within an average week? These are all investments in time which could be allocated to developing you as a better tool in the future.

High-Value Experiences

Finally, seek out opportunities for new experiences, especially those that are involved with technical expertise that you are not currently familiar with. This will give you an opportunity for continuous learning and will keep you challenged and learning.

Often you can make a deal with your employer in order to gain access to new tools or technologies. Offer to work with your organization to provide some individual learning time to a project in order to make it cost-effective to the organization. For example, my organization had wanted the new 3D printing technology for a long time. Not only did it come with a hefty price tag, but the learning curve was significant for the future operator. As we kicked this around for almost a year, our aggressive young technician offered to spend some of his personal time becoming familiar with the software and developing some of the early models. This became a win-win relationship for both the organization and the technician. The organization finally got access to the 3D printing technology that it had yearned for and that would help it go after new markets and demonstrate new competencies. The new technician, who will undoubtedly be very successful in the organization, now is the vehicle through which this new technology will be implemented, and is well positioned as someone within the organization to be developing the new technologies and high-value opportunities. This was a good investment of his time.

Other learning experiences fall into the same category. The de-facto standard for education in the past was that you climb on a plane, stay at an exotic place for a week, and obtain an expensive training (and bland food), and return home to rarely practice these new skills. In this new age, training is available at a discounted price, in bite-size chunks, and is as convenient as your computer (if you have taught yourself to learn through that medium). Certainly there are advantages to group classes with instructors, but many times you could learn just as effectively on an independent basis if you learn the discipline and skills to be able to learn from the new styles of learning technology.

While we are at it, all the knowledge that has ever been developed is available to you. If you could develop the competency to pick up a book, read it, organize, sort and synthesize the information and get high value from it, you will rarely need to take a class again. There is an art to being able to learn from a book, and you could learn it. Imagine how efficient you will be in the future if you could develop the competency to be able to read, organize and capture the important information from a book. Highly successful people have learned this skill—they don't spend time in classes; they spend their time effectively learning and experiencing a breadth of new ideas.

I've talked for a while here about developing your technical skills to be able to position you well for technical advancement and to instill good habits in order to allow you to use your time wisely and effectively. Next I will talk about what you should be learning about and begin to conceptualize a path forward for yourself beyond the acquisition of technical competence.

10 DEPTH VS. BREADTH

At the very beginning of your working career I encourage you to begin thinking about your career path and where you want to end up. The first five years of your career will significantly set your course for much of your future working career. A truck driver that sets out for a delivery, even across the nation, has his destination in mind when he departs. A boat captain not only has charted a course avoiding all unsafe areas but maximizing his route to avoid unfavorable currents and detours. In the same way, you can only maximize your efforts toward your career goal by making decisions that are in line with your plan.

Depth vs. Breadth
One of the initial questions that you will need to make will be whether your focus will be along the general trajectory of depth or breadth. Depending upon your field of practice, if you become very specific about the type of practice that you are exposed to, you could become very deep in your field during your initial technical experiences. You may think that this is great, and it may be very valuable to your employer. However it may limit your capability to either move into other project-related programs or to manage integrated projects, and may put you into a very narrow niche. If this is your desire, and this niche will be available and

viable throughout your working career you, may choose to dive in. However with career tracks such as the aerospace engineer, life is good when the economy is good and there are new airplanes to be designed and built, however it has proven to be a long and dry spell in-between.

It may pay you, then, to become a bit wider in your technical experience early in your career. As I have indicated your next career stage may include managing others on a project team with the goal of delivering a project to a customer. This would imply that a wider range of technical experiences would introduce you to a larger group within the organization and a broader experience base to draw from as a Project Manager. This wider experience would allow you to better understand the various roles that others have within the project team, how the deliverable would be measured and implemented more effectively, and to communicate the scope, progress and challenges of the project with the project team and the client.

Because there are many different professions and task assignments within the myriad of large and smaller organizations it is difficult to conceptualize all the possibilities within the context of this conversation. But what is important is to choose (or adapt) your work opportunities as best you can by engaging in work experiences which will lead you into the career trajectory that is important to you. Through effective planning and conceptualizing a path forward (at least generally) you are at least heading in the direction that you desire to move in, and that hopefully fits your skill sets and interests. If you have no map or plan, you end up wherever the road (or your employer) takes you, perhaps wherever the wind blows.

This also begs the concept of periodically taking stock of your progress and determining whether you are working effectively and satisfactorily toward your goals, or whether changes need to be made to the process or the methodology. It is also important to realize that the organization's environment changes, your own needs and interests change, your family situation changes and other opportunities may present themselves. Be aware of, open to and flexible enough to consider these options in order to continue to make decisions which are best for yourself and your family.

I'm always intrigued by the fact that universities will graduate you with the degree that interests you and that they have in their curriculum. They may not mention (or care) that there is a worldwide employment market for 100 of these degreed graduates. I mentioned the value of your skills to the market and that the need for these skills creates demand and the scarcity of these resources creates high value. In this day and age we are taught to follow our hearts and do the things that we enjoy doing. I would offer a different perspective—develop the skills and competencies which are valuable in the market (and that will be valuable in future markets) and maximize the return for your efforts, you can then use your spare time to do the things that you enjoy doing.

Environmental Change

Because the market that you enter into may not look at all like the market that you retire from, a more diverse technical focus may allow you to adapt to changing market conditions (unless, of course, your focus is at the heart of the new environmental trajectory). Because you may move into management and other higher-value positions as the profession's environment changes, adaptation may not be necessary. I'm just saying; don't get trapped into being the best buggy-whip-maker in the word.

To this point we have identified some early-career technical strategies for maximizing your initial career-building efforts. In the next section we will begin exploring some of the social and relational aspects of your career which will have long-standing effects on your effectiveness within the organization and local industry.

11 HELPING OTHERS & BUILDING RELATIONSHIPS

This is the point in your career when you have the opportunity to begin building your own private network. Now is when your peers and supervisors (and perhaps customers and others that you interact with) will gain their first impression of you. What will they see?

Human beings have an innate capacity for comparative analysis. We are always judging people, evaluating their appearance, performance and behaviors and inferring their value systems and perspectives from these observations. Some people come through high school and college with experiences which allow them to have more highly developed social skills; but most will be developing these skills continuously throughout their careers.

First Impressions

As the familiar saying goes, you never get a second chance to make a good first impression. If you join an organization new in your career experience, your co-workers will not expect you to be fully trained and capable of being able to perform at a professional level. Most likely they've been through the same processes that you have and generally know "where you are" in your professional journey.

What are they looking for in a new entrant?

Mostly they are looking for energy, drive, commitment and respect.

Energy

Energy is primary to having a fit life and will set the stage for health and success going forward. Energy is internally generated, and can be maximized through a healthy diet and lifestyle. One of my construction foremen told me, later in his life, that 'If I had known that I would live this long I would have taken better care of my body.' This fun statement, though, reflects on an important concept. Everything that you will be tomorrow is a result of what you do today.

Drive

Drive is that internal force that pushes you to keep striving for a goal. Early in your career you need to conceptualize your long-term and intermediate goals, and continue working toward those goals. Drive is highly valued in the business world. If you have a high level of internal motivation and drive for success your employer doesn't need to worry about keeping you busy— they just need to keep the target of these efforts properly directed.

Any un-occupied business time will be filled with whatever seems urgent at the time. If you have a goal that is important to you, you will need schedule time and effort to work toward it. When I was studying for my professional licensing exam and had a new wife and young children I spent about 6 months coming into work at 6 am. The hour that I had available on a daily basis allowed me to focus on the licensing requirements and examination. Since that time I have used similar strategies to plan for additional technical and professional licenses.

Find the time and personal discipline to identify, prioritize and work toward goals that are important to you. Communicating these goals and your effort toward them to others also reinforces your commitment to them, and helps sustain your focus. When I was working on my Ph. D. I didn't tell people for the first couple of years what the target of my studies was, for fear of failure. After I announced my intention it allowed others to support my striving toward my goal and their encouragement provided my support and motivated my efforts.

Commitment

Your peers, supervisors and others around you are interested in seeing you committed to achieving the goals of the group. This commitment is embodied by your attitudes, work efforts, and dedication to the task or work product. If you are working with a team it is really important to realize that your contribution is important to the goal, but that the team's product will only be successful if the entire team effort is successful. Just as the sports metaphor states 'There is no I in *team*' you need to support your other team members, be helpful and courteous and enable them to conceptualize their role and value to the success of the group. This attitude will go a long way in building relationships which will be important to you later in your career.

Self-control

People are interested in developing relationships that others that are consistent and worthy of respect. You need to be constantly aware of the things that you do consistently—they become your habits. You will be doing yourself a favor to develop a good friend (or spouse) who is not afraid to point out your habits and keep you alert. The further you go up your career ladder the more the little things affect your ability to be successful in social situations.

Begin shedding addictions and begin working toward the person that you want to be. First of all, there is no room in the modern workplace (or home) for illegal drugs. Tobacco is becoming socially unacceptable in many professional areas and is extremely detrimental to your health. If you have any respect for your future health and lifestyle, ditching the tobacco habit is a great place to start.

Self-control is the foundation for everything that you do in life. I mentioned working toward a goal, being consistent in your relationships, having integrity, developing respect, all of these stem from consistently behaving according to your personal goals and values. Develop an exercise regimen and healthy eating habits which will allow you to manage your weight at a comfortable level. Maintain a consistent energy level and drive. Monitor and control your alcohol consumption and behavior in public places. These will all contribute to your being capable of successful behaviors now and in the future, and ignoring these social cues can be a significant impediment toward your success.

Innovation

This term usually implies an organizational response toward embracing and working with new technologies, however I would offer that you can hold a personal position in personal advancement within or outside of the organizational relationship. Just as I discussed in the section on personal branding, you should have individual goals that may or may not align with the organization's goals. If these goals align long-term then you may stay with the organization and you both may both prosper together. If they are not in alignment, you may modify your goals in the future to adapt the organization's environment or you may influence the organization to change to come into alignment with your personal vision (especially later in your career as you are more able to influence the organization's position).

This begins with monitoring the environment and looking for new trends in the industry. Adapt the newest technology (whether financed by the organization or not) and begin using this technology to enhance your personal efficiency. Communicate these environmental trends to the organization's management and offer to help pilot some of these technologies within the organization, or establish a group of peers within the organization that would embrace these movements.

Because organizations (at least larger, staid organizations) tend to be run by older people mature in their careers, there are lots of opportunities for new innovative employees who have grown up with or educated using newer technologies to provide a lens for organizational growth and expansion. Proactive managers and leaders will be open to support and embrace these new technologies and opportunities as they play into the frames that they are familiar with and are affordable for the company.

People are Social Creatures

As I indicated before, a large part of your success will be related to your ability to work with, support and integrate with others within and outside of the organization. Thus it is important from the outset to be able to interact effectively with others.

The culture of the university has been shifting from a formal to an informal setting where learning, although programmed on a group basis, is embraced more on an individualized basis. Independence is exhibited in free-form clothing (jeans are ubiquitous) and shoes (if any) can be a myriad of bright colors and textures. Even professors are dressing down to the familiar forms of the students. Jumping into business organizations, however, means a shift to a different type of dress and behavior.

Depending upon where you are in the organization, expectations for behavior and dress may be flexible or more rigid. How you appear and dress is a personal reflection of yourself and how you want to be portrayed. Building on the previous comments about a personal brand and first impressions, if you are interested in being successful in the organization your goal should be to identify the acceptable appearances of your leaders and begin to emulate them. I am not saying you need to totally acquiesce to the 'cultural norm' of business dress, but I will say that people embrace and work with others that they feel comfortable with and believe that they understand, that fit with their 'norms'. The business community has fairly well established norms associated with dress, professional behavior and organizational hierarchy. Acknowledging these and adapting to them will help you be accepted and people to look favorably with respect to advancement and enhanced career opportunities.

Nothing kills the opportunity for success like not respecting the relationships and power systems within an organization. I would advocate treating everyone within the organization with respect, regardless of position. Sometimes, due to the informal power relationships with organizations, individuals with informal power are in unexpected places, so it is best initially to treat everyone with utmost respect (or at least until you can identify these informal power relationships).

The concept of treating everyone with respect is a great first step in developing deep relationships and maintaining personal humility. I have met new employees (and candidates) with a lack of humility and that trait almost assures that they will not be successful in achieving high organizational performance. If people work with them they keep their social distance and maintain these relationships on a plutonic level. A good dose of humility goes a long way, as does communicating to superiors with the appropriate respect level.

Successful people realize that they are never successful alone. Humility will allow you to be open to sharing the credit for the group's success with others on the team, your supervisor, and, if appropriate, your mentor. There will be many people along your initial career path that influence you in a positive way, and it is important to share your praise with them. This will provide rewards beyond the initial good feelings—people will know that they can trust you.

Team Player

Many of your initial projects will include others, and you can look around the organization and identify groups of people performing collectively. Success in these groups means sharing burdens (if someone else is having a problem delivering their portion of the project, how can you help). You must be perceived as someone that the team members can trust. This includes identifying the behavioral norms of the group and (if appropriate) accommodating to them. Showing respect for the power relationships within the team and how they measure success internally and externally should be acknowledged. The right amount of communication is important make the individuals in the group feel comfortable about you and your contribution and yet not appear to be self-centered. Again, a dash of humility goes a long way in a group setting.

Finally, if your group has a final product, the group is successful collectively only if the final product is acceptable. You may be acknowledged for your personal contribution, however if you can divert at least a portion of the praise for this success to the team you will develop significant credibility and trust.

Social Intelligence

Many of the processes that I have described above come under the broad headings of Emotional or Social Intelligence, which we will further develop in later chapters. I conceptualize Social Intelligence as the individual's ability to interpret the way that they are being conceptualized by others and be able to adapt their personal behavior in a way to be successful in the relationship. This includes understanding the social norms, power structures and expected behaviors in the organization and being able to adapt to them. Many careers have plateaued early because they were not able to identify and process these social cues, while most successful people have developed these social capabilities.

12 LEADERSHIP SKILLS

One of significant aspects of our personal development will be to lay the foundations of leadership early in our career. First of all, if you were not cooperative, friendly and a good follower earlier in your career people will not feel that you are worthy of working with and following in the future. Second, learning about and exercising leadership competencies early in your career will allow you to be successful in your current career position as well as building habits and behaviors that will help you develop and be successful in future leadership opportunities.

Being a Good Follower
As we begin our progress through our career stages you will learn about and begin to practice higher level leadership skillsets which will become more increasingly complicated, integrated and important toward reaching your goals. I talked earlier about leadership being an interaction between the leader, the follower(s) and the environment. At this level, however, let's consider learning leadership from the perspective of learning to be a good follower.

There are several things that you can do to begin learning about and understanding leadership concepts from a follower position. One of the first is to analyze the traits and behaviors of the people that you admire and that do (or perhaps those that don't) motivate you within and outside of the organization. Some of the greatest comedies on TV and in the movies are about organizations with managers ('leaders') that just don't understand appropriate social dynamics and are so self-centered that they are ineffective.

As a follower you have the opportunity to witness, interpret and understand organizational behavior and leadership traits from the ground up. Not everyone that you have as a supervisor motivates you, and you should train yourself to try to understand what it is about the behavior of the leaders that you admire (and those that you don't) and that motivates you to achieving the organization's goals (and perhaps your task goals) and strive for higher-level performance. These are skills that you should consider developing in yourself.

As an effective follower in the technical skills development portion of your career cycle there are a few key traits that you can begin to develop and exhibit which will help you grow an effective rapport with your leaders and your organizational peers.

The first falls under the heading of being a *facilitative leader*. When you are participating in a group project, are you helping others integrate, understand how their components work toward the whole and assisting people that are not able to complete their portion of the work efficiently? The facilitative leader can work at any level within the organization, helping other people complete their tasks and communicating difficulties in a manner that they can be supported or resolved.

Facilitative leaders are engaged in their work, and provide energy and support to the process. They are great team players and can be counted upon to meet their deadlines and help others to do the same. They are committed to the success of the group and the organization, not simply themselves. They don't have ulterior motives for their actions—they are interested in and committed to the group's success.

Next, good followers are *supportive* of the organization's and the leader's goals. You may not agree with all of the goals of the organization, but it is reasonable to assume that someone has put a lot of effort and thought into developing these goals. It is important to support these goals with all the energy and motivation as you can and be fair to watch and see if these goals prove to be effective. It is certainly counterproductive to an organization to have individuals or groups that are trying to undermine or circumvent important goals or processes within the organization. It is appropriate to provide feedback concerning your perspective of the goals, but once they are established or reinforced they should be pursued aggressively and without counter-productive ulterior motives. If your peers see that your efforts are not in alignment with the organization's goals, how will they feel about you when you are asked to assume a leadership position yourself?

Finally, as mentioned before, good followers are good *team players*. Closely aligned with the concept of a facilitative leader, effective team members realize that they cannot achieve the team's goals independently, and that there are a lot of team dynamics that can be positively (or negatively) influenced by the members. I will talk about teams in greater detail in the Professional Skills section of the book, so at this point it is important to realize that the teams succeed or fail as a team, and that a chain is only as strong as its weakest link. As a team member it is your responsibility to help organize, assist and support everyone's efforts toward the organization's goals. This should become the underlying tenant of your initial efforts on your leadership journey.

Core Values

Earlier when I talked about building your own personal 'brand' I introduced the concept of your character, and the fact that the behaviors exhibited by you are a reflection of these values that you hold dear. When people evaluate other people from a follower-leader perspective, one of the important criterions is whether they trust the leader. Is the leader working from a strong self-interest or does he have the follower and team's goals in mind? Do you trust him/her? Do their values lead them to make the correct decisions and support worthy goals?

How can you begin to become aware of your core values (those belief systems which you hold dear and that become the foundation of your behaviors and actions in the future)? From a Judeo-Christian tradition (that we hold in America) we hold the values of honesty, integrity, friendliness and having a good moral character to be in high esteem among those that we would feel comfortable working with and following. If we are going to begin looking at ourselves from the perspective of evaluating our core values, we need to understand the deep meaning of these terms.

Honesty is the condition that people are telling the truth (at least from the perspective that it is the truth as they understand it) and indicate how they have come to that position. They are sincere in their interest to express their beliefs to others and are not trying to deceive them or be manipulating them. This should be a fundamental canon in your behaviors with others—to be absolutely open and honest about your perspectives and opinions. You are attempting to build trust within those individuals that you work with. In the future they may not agree with your position, but if they feel that you are being sincere about the actions they will support them because they trust that you have the best intentions in mind and have a plan.

Closely aligned with honesty, *integrity* indicates that your beliefs and behavior will be based upon strong moral principles. If people feel that they will be dealt with fairly, are honestly represented, that their leaders care about them, and that their efforts are being expended to good ends they will be comfortable following them. Your actions early in your career will help establish the organization's perspectives about your motives and moral groundings. If you can communicate that you are an upstanding moral person, honest and empathetic to others, you will have established a foundation for deeper relationships and leadership values in the future.

A person's *character* is the outward expression of these attributes. A person's character is exhibited by their behavior. If a person holds high ethical ideals but does not follow through with them their character does not embody their alleged belief systems. One of the popular definitions that I like is that a person's character is what they do when nobody is looking.

Who are you and what do you stand for? People will be imputing and judging your character not from your espoused belief systems but from your actions. Do your behaviors follow your alleged belief systems; are they coherent in your actions?

Your peers will be watching and monitoring your behavior. They will be judging these actions by ethical and moral standards. Are you consistent, fair and transparent in your actions and intentions? Do you have the best intentions of others in mind or are you self-serving? Your actions will speak for you, and in order to guard against improper actions you need to be imbedding ethical norms into your thought processes. Once people feel that you have self-serving intentions, especially at the expense of others, it will be very hard to repair or get beyond these beliefs.

Perspective and Critical Thinking

One of the most important attributes, and most difficult to develop, is the ability to have a wider perspective. Through this book I have begun to explain the employment situation, careers, organizations and the environment from a metaphorical perspective. What are these things, how do they interrelate, what affects them, and how can we successfully work within them? *Perspective* allows you to step back and analyze the situation objectively.

Stephen Covey has a famous story about a group of people who are hacking their way through the jungle. One person climbs a tree to determine where they are heading and reports back that they are heading in the wrong direction. The response from the crew is that it doesn't matter—they are making great progress.

It is important to be able to develop the capacity to see situations and relationships objectively and within the context of the organization. So much of the time we have emotional ties to these relationships which cloud our ability to make rational judgments about the relative value of these relationships and future actions.

Critical thinking skills are those skill sets which allow us to make appropriate judgments about situations or relationships based upon balanced, accurate and correct information. Because the world is full of information it is often difficult to obtain high-quality, timely, un-biased and accurate information. Additionally, humans have flawed means of weighing and evaluating information and options, and develop biases and heuristic models for interpreting information. Given all of this, how can we develop processes for learning to think more critically?

Critical thinking begins with the understanding that we are a product of, and carry an underlying perspective of, our culture. Our culture is the collective of the values, beliefs and norms of the society in which we have grown up and live. Beginning with our early development we have internalized a set of common beliefs which have influenced who we are today, our value systems and how we organize and interpret information.

First, we are *biased* toward certain types and sources of information and away from others. Do we seek information from Fox News or National Public Radio (Television)? This pre-sorts some information and provides an interpretation of that information. In the same way history books are written by the groups that have won the wars in the past, the information that we have access to is sorted, interpreted and presented to us by some person or group. To understand the perspective that that group represents gives context to the information.

Second, we have processes through which we interpret this information—which are called *heuristics*. When we receive information about a car or truck we interpret this information based upon the types of vehicles that we are familiar with. We apply this to our standard conception of what these vehicles are, how they operate and what they look like. These heuristics are the 'boxes' that we interpret information against. Many professionals are trained to look at situations in accordance with these standard heuristics—when you see situation A you interpret the information in accordance with process B and come to conclusion C which is presented in a standardized format. We become comfortable with these processes and the standardization allows us to continually develop improved processes, standardize scientific improvements and communicate among professional groups using standardized processes.

A classic example of the big box during the initial development of computers was International Business Machines, or IBM. "Big Blue" conceptualized business machines in a larger scale and rigid business application. Microsoft (early in their organizational development) took the computer, added a graphical interface, and allowed it to be utilized the individual. To this day Google attempts to create environments where people can think outside the box, and Apple attempts to create products which are new and revolutionary.

The first part of 'thinking outside the box' begins with the realization that we exist in various boxes. We can begin by questioning the beliefs that we hold as 'true'. What is the basis of these sources of information? We hold family, religious, cultural and relational beliefs about what is good, bad, right, wrong, true or false. Until we begin to open our minds, experience different cultures, norms and expose ourselves to different patterns of information gathering, interpretation and judgment, we cannot begin to push the perimeter of our box.

Critical thinking processes drive us to questioning the very nature of our belief systems, understanding how we think and make conclusions, and to recognize these boundaries and beginning to work outside of these 'systems'. We need to begin to question the organizing framework of our perspectives and the validity of the information that we receive. Most of the information that we have access to was aggregated and in most cases interpreted for us. We need to understand the bias and motives behind the interpretation of this information, which allows us to begin to 'scrub' this information and obtain alternate information channels which will give us a different perspective of the 'data'. The following are some guidelines to begin examining our thought processes;

1. Our emotions and belief systems provide a major bias to our information processing. When we think about a rebel leader in an African country we usually don't attribute the same values to them as we do to Washington, Jefferson and Franklin in America's history. Become more aware of the effect our emotions have on our information interpretation.
2. How we process data should be stripped from our assumptions and prejudices in order to be able to give it critical analysis. Our view of the world (and subsequent perspectives on information about the world) should be based upon the way that it is as opposed to the way that we want it to be or think that it should be.
3. Next, we should get as close to the raw data as possible so that we can interpret the data ourselves (presuming we have the capacity

to do so) as opposed to obtaining that information pre-sorted and interpreted for us.
4. Finally, we need to question the source of the data and the interpretation of the data. Who prepared the information and formulated the conclusions. Is the information collected in accordance with appropriate scientific processes, interpreted in an un-based manner and printed in a peer-reviewed periodical? What reasons do they have for presenting the information as they did? Is there motivation for presenting the interpretation that they have?

The goal of this process is to increase awareness of the influence that we and others introduce into the information that we use for our decisional and interpretation processes. This allows us to be more aware of our thinking processes, validity of the information that we are using for our decision making and interpretation, and understanding our behaviors based upon these elective (and perhaps re-interpreted) norms.[ii]

Emotional Intelligence

We will further discuss Emotional Intelligence later in the book; however it is important to be on the radar screen of new professionals and others on a growing career trajectory. Research in psychology indicates that there are several types of intelligences or different cognitive processing strengths that are being teased apart. Everyone is familiar with the generalized measurement, or g, which is an expression of a broad-based cognitive processing ability in the areas being tested. There is no general agreement about the validity of the measurement of EQ nor whether it is a real form of intelligence, but for our purposes it serves to highlight traits that you should be aware of at this point in your career development.

Emotional intelligence is a component of our intellect which deals with our processing of emotional data. I like Salovey & Mayer's[iii] definition which recognizes that "individuals vary in their ability to process information of an emotional nature, and in their ability to relate emotional processing to a wider cognition". Thus if you are high in emotional intelligence you have a higher ability to identify your emotional contribution to your thinking processes, assess the role of these contributions and have some level of control over the processing of this emotional content. As we earlier discussed critical thinking processes in the identification and qualification of information for our understanding and decision making, the role of emotional intelligence is helpful in our understanding of how our emotions affect our behavior and decision making.

At this point in your career, it is important to become aware of the way that your emotions affect your thinking processes and relationships development. You should become more aware of your own and other people's emotions and how those emotions influence your and their decision processes. Through the development of this awareness, you may be able to influence your own productivity by being aware of your feelings about the tasks at hand. Additionally, other people are processing this emotional content as well, and if you can help them understand the situation and the role that their emotions are playing in their decisions and behaviors then they can be guided into more adaptive and positive behaviors. Goleman[iv] has written several books about identifying and using emotional intelligence which may be helpful in the development of a background understanding of EI and the role that emotions play in our thinking processes.

Self-regulation

Bridging several of these concepts, self-regulation skills are important to our emotional well-being. Self-regulation is the ability to act in ways that are consistent with your value systems, what would appear as similar to our perspective of character. This behavior would allow a person to be comfortable with their actions, avoiding negative feelings such as guilt or anxiety. When applied to the emotions, self-regulation allows you to calm yourself down when you become frustrated.

Many times we are frustrated from achieving our goals (be it small like interrupting our schedule or a significant event in our lives). This creates a tension at the subconscious level which in turn triggers a negative emotional response on a conscious level. When we are frustrated in our ability to accomplish our goal, this triggers emotional processing and blocks our ability to think clearly and respond rationally.

If you are able to self-regulate you can remain calm (or calm yourself down), step back and analyze the situation, and process an appropriate response. You would also have the ability to emotionally pick yourself up when you are down. In the working world, and especially in high stress situations, you may have very little control over the situation at the time. If you have developed self-regulating skills, however, *you can control your emotional response to the situation*, and in turn make better decisions or take more effective action.

This begins with an awareness of your emotional response to situations. It is helpful to analyze situations where there was a high emotional response from you. Did the emotional response block you from thinking clearly, determining or taking an appropriate action going forward? Through a process ongoing analysis you can begin to understand the role that emotion plays in your responses. You can also begin to conceptualize the scenario where you would respond differently to these situations and the resulting emotional tags that are attached to them. This will help you position yourself to have a different response where your rational processing can allow you to minimize the emotional content and leave more opportunity for an effective response.

Passion

Try to develop and organize your work situation (the tasks, the ways that the tasks are implemented or the outcomes) so that you are able to be passionate about what you do. If you are able to identify with the positive aspects of your work, the tasks or the outcome you will have a higher sense of satisfaction about your job, enjoy lower stress levels, and have a higher sense of satisfaction about your job. These positive feelings translate out of your work life and into your home life as well, just as problems and frustrations at home affect your relationships and attitudes at work.

If you can focus on the positive aspects of your job and envision new and innovative ways to perform the work and become more efficient at it, you will be happier at work and exhibit a positive mental attitude. These types of attitudes can be contagious, both at work and at home.

Develop a healthy lifestyle

I would encourage you to develop healthy living habits early in your life and strive to maintain them over time. There are many lifestyle books and information available, so I won't go into great detail here, but there are a couple of important aspects that should be emphasized.

First, is diet—learn to eat a healthy diet. It can be easy to get into the "burger" mode, and have your lunches on the fly. What you eat for breakfast drives your energy level through lunch, what you have for lunch sets the pace for the afternoon, and your evening meal gets digested while you wind down and sleep. Your larger meals at breakfast and tapering at lunch will provide the energy through the normal workday. Hone in what is normal for you, and find your 'balance'.

Exercise is important to develop and

maintain the muscles and tone that you will need throughout your life. I'm not saying you need to run marathons, although that is a worthy goal. It does mean that you should find things that you enjoy doing that provide moderate levels of exercise and cardio-pulmonary engagement. Develop an exercise routine that you enjoy and that is an easy process to engage in and dovetail with your work activities. It also is important to find something that your spouse/significant other is interested in as well, if that is possible. If you do things together you will not have the stress of having to trade off one time for another.

Stress is another factor that you will need to learn to deal with successfully. As you went through college you may have experienced stressful situations. Stress is your body's way of dealing with deadlines, pressure and other 'threats'. Stress response to these pressures is pretty much hard-wired into us. It is triggered by the way that we *interpret* pressure in our lives. A little bit of pressure is good in that it triggers a background emotional response which energizes us and provides energy to get the target activities completed.

Too much stress, however, can provide significant health problems down the road (and not very far down the road if your family is pre-disposed to hypertension (high blood pressure) and other health conditions). For some people a combination of stress and bad eating habits can be a deadly combination.

How should you learn to deal with stress? As I initially indicated, stress is your body's response to the perceived threats in your life. These can be personal threats (troubling time with a spouse/friend) or work-related stress (deadlines, work quality, customer challenges). It is important to keep in mind what is really important at the particular time and to 'process' these situations appropriately. Unfortunately, this is incredibly difficult, especially during highly stressful situations, because the emotional processing portion of the brain can overdrive a lot of the cognitive processing capacity, so it is not possible for you to think clearly. Having a good person available to act as a sounding board to bounce some of these situations off of is important so that clear perspective of a situation can be visualized and an appropriate response developed.

On normal days, the best way to deal with a potentially stressful situation is to take a few minutes and re-conceptualize the situation. What is really going on? Is it important or does it just seem urgent? Is it appropriate that I respond emotionally? Many times a stressful day is a combination of things that push you over a tipping point. If you can, disconnect from the situation for a while and discuss it with a level-headed friend. Another benefit of exercise is that it allows you to release the adrenalin that is built up in your body during a stressful period.

Gossip
Gossip, spreading rumors or idle talk should be avoided in the professional workplace. Unless you have direct information and are authorized to

share this information, gossip is often considered irresponsible at the low level and at the high end a passive form of workplace violence or dominance. Using social media to communicate about professional matters is always inappropriate while using email to communicate any type of inappropriate or personal information is highly un-professional and, because of the permanence of these types of media, poses a risk to you personally or professionally. A great litmus test goes beyond the 'grandmother test' and poses the question 'Would you like to see what you are about to send on the front page of the paper tomorrow?'

In this section I have shown what you may expect to experience in an initial technical role within an organization, and how you can utilize the time to optimize your experiences, capabilities and personal abilities and conceptualize and hone your value system. With the development of these skills you will be better prepared for your future experiences. In the following sections I will look into the next career stage—the development and exercising of professional skills.

Professional Skills

13 PROJECT MANAGEMENT

Our goal during the phase of Technical Skills phase of our career trajectory is to acquire and hone our technical skills. During that period you have learned about the technical aspects of your profession or field, understand how it is regulated, and have perhaps achieved a technical or professional certification. You may have spent time interfacing with the client or had project-related responsibilities. You have spent time with a team that has delivered a project and seen how other areas have integrated to provide a complete product for a client.

During the next phase of your career development you will be developing what I will refer to as your professional skills. This includes the competencies of:

- Project Management: planning, staffing, managing and delivering a complete project. This will become conceptualized as an integrated process, bringing together multiple groups and players to achieve a common goal.
- Understanding your clients, what they want, and how to please them.
- How to build, motivate and energize a project team.
- Leadership at the project level—what skills will allow you to become successful in the

management and delivery of projects or services.

In the following section we will begin to conceptualize the things that we do as a project or production process.

Production Orientation

In a production situation there will be standardized processes which, when performed consistently, will provide a high quality product. In an industrial process various parameters will be measured to assure that the process is performed with minimal variation, and this variation is tracked and compared with the baseline to predict error rates or defects. New products or innovations are normally created through a research and development process while minor process refinements happen on an incremental basis on the process floor.

This conception is helpful for ongoing processes such as those you would find in the health care industry. Although the identification of problems and specific care is sometime subjective, the processes of treatment, cleanliness and protocol are very refined.

Project Orientation

In a project-related situation the product is usually unique and perhaps has never been done before. This requires a unique solution to the problem and requires a team to plan, organize and implement the solution and execute the project to produce the product or service. Projects can happen in accordance with fixed processes, which we will discuss; however the finished product or service is unique. At the end of the project the participants will be released from the project (and hopefully have another project to be moving to). Construction, engineering, computer software development, and other similar processes are examples of these types of projects.

The conceptualization of your organization's processes as production or project-related can be helpful in your understanding of the goals and methods of your organization and understanding what skillsets will be important for you to develop and refine during your professional development. You will be more valuable to the organization as your skills and capabilities are in line with the organization's needs.

Project Management

Project Management is the process of identifying, organizing, controlling and delivering a product or service in a project environment. This includes identifying and controlling the project's scope, budget, schedule, risk and understanding among the project's stakeholders. (Stakeholders are people that are affected by the project—employees, clients, suppliers and sometimes others in the community). Project Managers are concerned with (and responsible for) the flow of all the activities required to bring the project together and deliver the product.

In the previous section we learned to develop the processes which would help us be successful in the mastery of the technical and regulatory aspects of our career. This dealt with strict attention to the technical details and processes associated with the profession. In this section the skills that allowed you to be successful do not easily translate into managing project delivery. In fact, the successful Project Manager (PM) is a generalist and is responsible for monitoring and managing the flow of several processes in order to have the project completed successfully.

As we talk about the Project Management processes and the skills required to be effective through these processes, we want to recognize that more complicated processes have multiple projects operating simultaneously, and a PM (or Program Manager in a more complicated process) may be managing multiple aspects of different projects at the same time. For example, if an engineer is managing a construction project there may be an Architect working on the project design, a contractor performing preliminary construction activities and others within the organization ordering and staging materials to arrive at strategic points in the project. In this situation, the ability to see the big picture, analyze multiple information sources and manage multiple teams and contractors operating in parallel.

The following is an overview of the project management processes, as organized by the Project Management Association's *Project Management Body of Knowledge (PMBOK)*:
1. Project *initiation* includes development of the project overview document, called the

Project Charter, which includes the requirements for the project or service to be produced (deliverable) and identifying a high level budget and schedule. These may have been prepared using minimal design and resources. The project becomes a project when the Charter is accepted and funded.

    a. Individuals that are developing this must have well-developed skills for conceptualizing the client's needs, communicating clearly, conceptualizing a budget and being comfortable proceeding with a concept and without knowing all the information which will be developed later in the project. Sensitivity to a client's understanding of the project outcome, delivery process and communication needs is vital to being able to deliver a project in a comfortable manner to the client which meets their needs.

2. *Planning* includes the processes associated with taking the Charter and "fleshing it out," creating a full project plan. This plan, when completed, will have a well-defined scope and product requirements, a budget which includes enough information to meet the owner's requirements, and an expectation of when the final product (and intermediate milestones) will take place. The plan will have a staffing plan indicating how the work

will be completed, and an understanding of the risks that could lead to unplanned events during the project's execution. This end of the planning process will have another phase-gate, or an opportunity for the Project Team and the Owner to make sure that the project goals are still worth the project expense.

    a. Obviously the skill sets necessary for carrying out the planning process includes the ability to conceptualize the whole project flow, organize technical people to provide their contribution to the scope document, budgeting, conceptualizing the project flow in the form of a schedule, understanding the client and the environment well enough to identify and communicate project risk, and manage all these components together to provide a holistic project concept and the ability to communicate this concept clearly.

3. The project *execution* phase is the phase of the project where the work is actually completed. Materials are procured and staged for delivery, and equipment is rented, purchased and/or leased for the project. Also in this section the project team is acquired, trained, gets together and executes the project.

a. This phase of the project requires to the PM to have the ability to communicate clearly among the client, project team and other key stakeholders. The PM also manages the expectations of the project team and the client among multiple communication channels. Complicated projects with multiple groups often have project coordination meetings that bring the main players together periodically to make sure that everyone is working efficiently and effectively toward the goal. Often projects have a communication plan which organizes the information collection, processing and distribution to important stakeholders within multiple organizations.

b. The PM also needs to manage the interpersonal dynamics of the project team. Team dynamics in a project environment can be challenging. If the project is time-constrained or financially-constrained then this can provide additional burdens on the team and require additional time and skills managing these problems. The group dynamics of forming, storming, norming, performing and adjourning should be familiar to the PM and other group leaders.

    c. The execution phase of the project is completed when the project is delivered to the client and the client accepts this delivery as fulfillment of the contract. Sometimes the PM becomes the 'negotiator' with the client to determine when the project is completed or 'substantially complete' and allows the PM to begin the closing process.
4. The *monitoring and controlling* aspects of the PM's responsibilities include making sure that the project's members are performing in accordance with the plan, that the finances are running in accordance with the budget, and that the project will be completed in the appropriate time frame. If the project is not achieving these goals it is the PM (and his team) to exercise corrective measures to put the project back on track with the client's expectations or manage change to the organization's scope to allow for this variance.

    a. Because change happens, the PM is responsible to manage project change and keep all the important stakeholders aware of potential scope movement. Sometimes information comes available during the project execution which requires scope change, and it is the responsibility of the PM to make sure that scope change is managed properly in a coordinated manner. The PM makes sure that project change is properly authorized by the client, and that attendant cost, schedule and risk accommodation is considered in the scope change.

b. The PM needs to have enough experience (or have the resources to assist him) in the management of project risk. Understanding project risk—unplanned events which affect the project—is vital to the effective Risk Management on a project. Being open to un-planned events can allow an agile company to take advantage of opportunities and minimize the impact of negative events.

c. The PM needs to understand the processes being performed well enough to be able to determine whether the intermediate milestones are being met and that the intermediate deliverables are will meet the project's goals. The understanding of the organization's (and client's) quality control programs and determining whether the deliverables and production is within these guidelines is an important aspect of the PM's coordination duties.

d. The PM needs to be able to understand and coordinate the project's finances and projections to assure that the project's financial (and, closely related, the project's schedule) performance is within the range of expectations of the project. Deviations from the project's budget and schedule need to be managed by a correction plan.
5. The project *closing sequence* of activities is the portion of the project where the team completes all related contract responsibilities (documentation, as-built drawings, project archiving), disbanding the project team, satisfying the client. Sometimes there are personal dynamics which need to be managed associated with disbanding (or hopefully reassigning) the project team members.
6. Throughout these sequences project scheduling is vital. All the team members, procurement, subcontractors and the client's activities all need to be carefully sequenced, monitored and arranged (sometimes at the project site) to allow for an efficient and orderly project delivery. This takes coordination at a task level and the ability to maintain a high-level picture. When things happen to create conflicts to a project the PM needs to take appropriate action to adjust the schedule and activities to accommodate the deviation.

a. This requires the ability to look at the project from a multitude of dimensions—scheduling and sequencing. Basic working knowledge about project scheduling, drivers for change and issues that could cause deviations in the scheduling should be understood at a tacit level. Maintaining sequencing and project workflow is almost as much of an art as it is a science.
7. Throughout the project the project budget needs to be managed. The client has a certain expectation about the expected project costs, and as the project is delivered and variance accrues, it needs to be controlled against the project contingencies.
a. This requires an understanding of the project budget drivers, unit costs and how changes to the scope and schedule affect the budget. Skills include understanding the financial tools associated with the project budget tracking and variance. As the project is executed the project budget needs to be updated to allow variance from the earned value to be tracked and new projections made periodically updating the client and the management team's expectations.

What should be very obvious from the above sequence of activities and skill sets is that few of these are directly related to (and thus built upon) the technical tasks that you have been expected to master during the Technical Skills phase of your career. Hopefully as you perfected your technical skills were looking ahead and trying to understand the dynamics of project (or production) delivery so that you were more prepared as you moved into the Professional Phase of your career.

14 CLIENT FOCUS

It's been very interesting to me that young professionals, as they learn the technical aspects of product or service delivery in their particular field develop their own perspectives about how these services should be delivered and what value is. These concepts are learned through the development of their skills and processes on the technical side and from their peers and managers. These perspectives comprise the service delivery while they are developing their technical skills, based upon their manager. Once you enter into the Professional Skills portion of your career, you will be interfacing more with the client directly, identifying what their needs are and how your services can be tailored to their needs.

We become programmed about delivering the pre-programmed services to our client because that is what we learned and have become used to providing. Sometimes the professional environment puts a box around the 'deliverables' and requires them to be a particular format and organization. Where there is flexibility in the product and through the service delivery process you have a chance to customize your delivery to meet your client's requirements and perhaps make them happy.

Identify Client's Needs
By this time you may be familiar with your

industry's standard products and services, but are you familiar with your client's needs? Their needs may be in line with the standard issue products, but they may not. How could their unique needs be identified and met? How could they perhaps be exceeded?

I had an opportunity to meet with a representative from the financial industry the other day, and this was certainly not a new experience for me. After the usual pleasantries they pulled out a binder that had been especially prepared for me. They had done their homework and new that I was an organizational freak, and they nailed me with their presentation, and anticipated my needs and provided a package that was right up my alley. I even went home and showed my wife the new binder and she said "well they nailed you, didn't they. You must be very happy right now."

How can you learn so much about your client that you blow them away? It doesn't need to be anything spectacular, and they may have understood much about me from my demographics, but they put the extra effort in to understand my desires instead of pitching their standard package. They made me feel special, and in return bought a lot of goodwill.

Talk to Your Client

It is certainly important to talk to your client throughout the project, but there are a couple of critical times when you should be asking pointed questions and trying to understand their perspectives and what they value. These opportunities are at the beginning (and sometimes before the beginning) of the project or the service delivery and at the end.

As you start a project, how do you know what the customer really wants? In many industries professional services are likely to be somewhat standardized products. The real question to understand is what does the client understand or value either in the final product or in the delivery of this product? In your service delivery, what would provide extraordinary value for the client—make them say 'wow' (at least under their breath).

When I am interviewing for a project I make sure that I let the client talk as long as they are willing to about the product or service that they want to receive. You wouldn't believe how easy it is to come in with PowerPoint presentations blazing and go on for an hour talking about the types of things that we have done for other clients in the same areas. It is more difficult to slow the process down and ask deep questions about how services have been provided in the past and what they liked and did not like. This is often a good way to begin developing a new relationship with a client.

If they are going to get the same (or nearly the same) product from other professionals, see if you can get them to let you know what they value about the service or delivery. How can we deliver these services in a way that would allow them to be really appreciated by the client? What are examples of great experiences in the past and what did they not like about other professional products or services?

There is also a significant component of education which needs to take place between the professional and the client. Often we understand the environmental, regulatory and standardized processes for service delivery, however our client may not. How can we determine where they are and make sure they understand the important aspects of our project/service delivery and what to expect through the process. It can certainly save a lot of headaches and, if done well, provide a lot of value with the client.

Lessons Learned

After completing your projects, it's important to sit down with the client and the team and ask them what they liked about the project or its delivery and what they didn't like. Having a checklist or guideline will help to ask the probing questions which will dig out the experiences that have been buried in time. Ask questions about the financial, timing and communications of the project delivery.

Your goal here is two-fold. The first is to identify things that your organization can improve upon. These lessons and improvements need to be taken back and processed by your company. How can your organization improve its delivery in these areas that the client identified (and also your own internally identified improvements from your own Lessons Learned processes)? Because making changes within an organization is often difficult, having top management supporting the lessons learned process and organizational adaptation around continuous improvement helps institutionalize changes that are suggested by the client.

The second goal is to identify the nuances and "personality" of the client. Just as individuals are very different from each other, so are organizations. The organization's personality is its "culture", and these cultures differ in both their value systems and their preferences. Adapting your services for each of the clients individually will allow you to build deep relationships with them. Sometimes these organizations bring their own standards for delivery processes or finished products. Understanding these processes and adapting to them is usually the foundation of a good relationship.

Another important thing to consider is that you are usually delivering these products to a particular person in the organization. If this point person is able to influence future purchasing decisions it makes sense to understand their individual needs, concerns and preferences. In the past some of my clients have been interested in "making my problems go away." They are stressed, busy and often interested in having time to go home and spend time with their family. At that point my focus was to find a way to efficiently operate autonomously and to report my progress and communicate with that manager in a way that allowed minimal interaction, and often where they could send my communication on with their own report and it minimized their personal time and involvement. Little tricks like this can often help you build deep relationships with the client.

Make Them Happy

Ultimately, the client (or potential client) is an individual or organization full of individuals. To this end they operate on two different levels. Usually the 'organization' is happy when projects or services are delivered in accordance with their requirements at a reasonable cost, in accordance with the expected schedule, and in alignment with their own standard processes.

The individuals in the organization often have different goals. Some are interested in moving up in the organization, some are interested in looking around, and some are interested in going home after an 8 or 10 hour day. Spending some time cueing in on the individual (or group) that you need to satisfy will help you understand how to tweak your product or service to meet their individual needs and goals, and 'make them happy.'

Organizational Culture

Thinking ahead to the time when you will be able to manage or influence your organization's direction and focus, imagine how things might be done differently within your organization if their goals were focused on client satisfaction. What if the organization's delivery processes were adaptable to each client's interests. What if the focus of each individual's activities on a daily basis was to make the corresponding person in the client's organization 'happy'? How would that change the way services were delivered to the customer? How would that change the way people feel in your organization?

    Now you have an opportunity to begin identifying your clients' needs and interests and customizing your services toward accommodating them on the micro-level. Someday when you get an opportunity influence the organization's culture on a macro-level, you can begin to help define (or refine) the organization's focus toward the concept of the clients' satisfaction. Falling under the umbrella of 'customer service' or 'customer satisfaction' there could be a higher level to strive for—'customer pleasure'?

15 TEAM FOCUS

It is people that do the work of planning, preparing, and providing products or services for their clients. The better and more efficiently they are able to provide these services the higher the satisfaction is among clients and the higher quality clients will be attracted in the future. It seems that our goal, then, should be to attract and train high quality individuals to our teams, train them effectively and encourage high performance in alignment with the client's needs. Sounds simple, right?

Interestingly, we live in an age of increasing specialization. Through the technical portion of your career you balanced the need for depth (specialization in a narrow field of study) vs. breadth (specialization across a wider spectrum of topics with less of an in-depth understanding of a particular area). In the professional role you are transitioning into a role of organizing other technical employees toward the completion of a product or service. Hopefully the following sections will help you understand the dynamics of individuals working together and how to optimize their performance.

Groups and Teams
Groups of people come together for a common purpose. They could share a very narrow

interest or be aligned in a common destiny. It is interesting to consider the various groups that we participate in. The largest is our national citizenship. People came together years ago for mutual protection, the preservation of our rights and common utility (we don't have to build the road in front of our house, produce our own electricity or pump our own water). We have been allocated into this group because of the location and/or association of our parents. We maintain our position within this group by behaving within the regulated 'norms' of the group. You are also a member of your community, church and employment organization. You have chosen to belong to these groups because of the mutual benefits from them that are appealing to you. You have the choice to operate, again, within the 'norms' of the group or to leave the group and pick another group in which to participate.

Consider other groups with which you have a looser affiliation. Other organizations to which you may come and go—the NRA, Sierra Club, Ducks Unlimited, Greenpeace, Rotary Club, your college's alumni association and a myriad of others. Sometimes we come and go within these organizations and participate as we feel an affiliation to them based upon our current thoughts and feelings. It is much easier to come and go in these groups and our participation in them can be very limited or significant as we choose.

Teams, in my definition, are a special subset of groups. In the case of teams, the individuals within the group will be successful only if the final product of the group is successful. An example of the team participation could be the production of a software product. If you consider the conceptualization, user interface, data collection, storage, retrieval and presentation, operating platform and deployment of the software, a deficiency in any one of these areas will provide a deficient product and affect the performance of (and perhaps the viability of) the finished product and perhaps the organization.

The sports metaphor of this is the football team. I the true sense of the meaning of the word 'team', when two teams are vying for the Superbowl, only one team will win, and the collective rewards for the individuals on the team are significant. They will share these rewards only if the team collectively beats the other team. There may be an outstanding player that is acknowledged for their performance, but their rewards are largely due to their collective participation. Between seasons they can choose to pool their skills with different teams if they choose to, but once they join the team they are usually there for at least a season.

Although they use the same word, an Olympic 'team' would not always qualify for my intended meaning. Individual sports participants may group together for training and to challenge each other in a world-class fashion, however they may achieve success on an individual basis. Although there is an esprit de corps among the individual participants, they often will achieve ultimate success through outperforming their own teammates.

Many of the projects that you work on will be successful through the group efforts of the other individuals within the group. The individuals within a team can get individualized rewards, however the successful performance of the team (delivering the high-value product or service) will provide the basis for the rewards for individual and group performance.

In many professional organizations which are termed 'projectized organizations', and especially larger ones, individuals come together in teams to perform projects and then move to other teams. In fact, they may belong to multiple project teams simultaneously, and this may appear to be a continuous production process for multiple stakeholders. I believe it is helpful, though, to maintain the team and project mentality in that it provides a clear mental path toward providing a product for a client and measuring their satisfaction with the product and/or service. Finally, it allows us to identify and correct defects in the project delivery process and correct it in the future.

Team Dynamics

As you watched teams work and participated in them through your technical skills development phase, you had an opportunity to see how the team dynamics operate. As you watched new members join project teams you may have witnessed their observation of the team, dynamics, and slowly increased and adapted their participation in the team.

Teams get together, develop patterns for

smooth operation and become effective in a generally prescribed manner. *Forming* describes the early stages where group members (and new entrants to the group) are trying to 'gel' together, understand the other individuals, and understand the accepted norms of the group. These can include who is formally (or informally) in charge, who the gatekeepers are, the prescribed order of activities, behaviors that are expected to be shown and appropriate protocols. The process described as *storming* indicates that during the initial phases of the development of a project team there can be period of time where the processes are challenged and the boundaries of the 'norms' of the group can be tested. During this *norming* period the behaviors, protocol and respect is established among the group.

Now that the group has established their focus and acceptance of the group norms they begin *performing* effectively as a group. This is the time that they will be productive and efficient in the production and delivery of the product. Finally the *closing* processes include the completion of the project, final documentation and archiving, and termination of the group.

If teams come together for subsequent projects they have the opportunity to skip through some of the earlier group processes because they know each other and standards for behavior, and have the opportunity to jump into the 'performing' processes.

Team Behaviors
Older groups have established their norms of

interpersonal working relationships, and have established their working culture. Introducing new methods and concepts can be met with resistance if these ideas are not introduced diplomatically, tactfully and thoughtfully. People in teams feel each other out, find out how the others want to be interfaced with and how they want to be treated.

One big norm is that of humor and playing around. Some people enjoy humorous situations and gentle poking; others can appreciate it or tolerate it. Once these expectations are understood by the group they become more comfortable with each other and can have fun together.

An important dynamic in getting teams to work well together is to have them all realize the value of the contribution of others. Having them appreciate the roles that they each play develops the respect of the group for each other and what they bring to the table. This is especially important as they work together in multiple situations.

Gossip and in-fighting can ruin a group. As a group leader or manager of a group, always have positive things to say about the contributions of the group members. They need to know that you care and appreciate and will support them. If you get down on a single individual within the group they will assume that you will pick on each of them if you have a chance. Thus, discipline should always happen tactfully and in private.

As you can, find a way to reward the group's performance and behavior as a team. Find things to reward them collectively. It is OK to celebrate an individual once in a while but keep it balanced and make sure that the team is appreciated and that they don't sense any favoritism.

Set a good example for team behavior. Make sure that everyone is contributing to the product of the team and that the process is flowing as it should. You should have some sort of measurement and feedback system for the workflow of the team and allow each of the members to see and understand their role and when their contribution is expected. Many of the team members will pick up on the work of others if something needed to be completed at a particular time and it is not. Having someone accomplish the tasks of another within the group just reinforces that behavior in the future. (Obviously the exception to this would be if a team member was unable to complete a task and the others agreed in this situation to support them.)

Projectized Organization

A projectized organization can be conceptualized as organization where their output is a multitude of individual project outputs. Within these organizations there are technical disciplines, but most value is delivered through a process of ongoing one-off projects. From the this outline, it is obvious that groups that work together on a repeated basis on similar projects will become increasingly efficient because they have established norms for working together and for the collective output of the team. They can thus expend the additional project effort identifying means to improve their project delivery processes.

Also, I mentioned that within a projectized

organization, teams often form to create a product or service then disband to form other teams to deliver other projects. This process can include many overlapping projects which are delivered for different clients with different needs and wants. It is the responsibility of the project manager to manage the dynamics of the project team and provide project outputs from the various project teams that are customized for (or at least meet the unique requirements of) the particular customer. This emphasizes the need for organizational standards for project delivery which dovetail with the industry's standard processes.

      Different groups also vary in their need for collaborative effort and communication. Groups that have worked together in the past may require minimal overlapping communication and may have developed shortcut processes to standardize this communication. Groups which have never worked together before or groups with new entrants will need guidance and direction in assuring that the correct amount of and appropriately timed communication will allow for effective project flow. Often scheduling the information flow is important to production efficiency, and in the absence of this, frequent meetings can facilitate or trigger the need for information from other group members at appropriate times.

      Meetings, when held, should follow logical patterns and be as efficient as possible. They should have minutes or standardized formats to allow for the participants to gather and stage the information beforehand and present this information as efficiently as possible. Someone should be taking notes—any meeting important enough to gather the team together should document the outcomes unless the information which is communicated is the outcome of the meeting. Documentation of the meeting puts everyone on the same page and provides the 'collective memory' of the group and activity at the time of the meeting. These should have action items—the agreed-upon activities of various members in order to move the project forward.

Individual Interaction

Groups are comprised of individuals, and these individuals will have different preferences as to how they would like to be communicated with, norms and processes within the group, and expectations. Groups collectively will build norms around the individuals, and the PM should be in a position to monitor the information flow and individual preferences and make sure that the groups and the individuals perform effectively. Interactions among individuals should at least be on a professional level and hopefully the individuals will get to know themselves individually and adapt their communication interaction and processes to be compatible with others within the group.

Synergy vs. Competition

Wherever possible, project teams should have their goals aligned and you should do your best not to get the individuals into a perceived competitive environment. An efficient team works collaboratively, watching the others and dovetails their efforts with others and the changing needs of the project and individuals. Just as a basketball team is adaptive to the opponent's position and approach and their own teammate's movements and actions, good team processes in a professional environment could take on many of the same processes. If some team members are stressed and it is a familiar process, others could step in to support the busy member and support their activities. There needs to be open and transparent communication to allow for this mutual support and synergy.

    We will work on teambuilding and encouraging processes more in the Leadership Skills section of this book (Chapter 20).

16 WORK MOTIVATION AND DRIVE

As you are working with and managing groups of people toward their goals, it is important to develop a basic understanding of motivation and, more specifically, work motivation—what makes people put extra-ordinary effort forth toward the goals of the manager or the group. I will begin the discussion with an introduction of the concept of motivation itself.

Motivation, at its simplest form, is a drive (desire to put energy forth) toward a particular goal. Humans have goals on both the subconscious level (for example, hunger, thirst, desire, empathy) and the conscious level. Subconscious level drives (or those below the level of perception) are based upon hereditary attributes and learned patterns of responses. Conscious level motivations and behaviors are based upon the individual's evaluation of their own personal needs, environmental factors, previous experience, and comparison with other individuals. A few important concepts around human motivation are that:
1. Individuals experience multiple motivating drives at different times, and that many are simultaneously experienced,
2. These drives happen both above and below the conscious level, that

3. these drives can be internally motivated, provided by the environment, or conceived or fabricated by the individual,
4. These drives produce action of the individual toward the goal, and
5. The perception of progress toward the goal, weighed against the acuteness (or value) of the need and the effort put forth, provide the motivating drive *at that particular time*.

We will use these concepts to build a model of motivation that will be helpful to us moving forward. Essentially, when we see something that we need (or want) we make an effort to acquire the object of our attention. This is the fundamental aspect of work motivation that we will attempt to understand.

Work Motivation

There are several prominent theories which variously attempt to describe or predict the motivation that an employee would have toward a work-related goal. Without an exhausting evaluation of these theories, there are several aspects of these theories which would be helpful to understand at this point.

1. Employees provide their work efforts to the organization in an exchange process, and in return expect to receive valued outcomes. These outcomes can be extrinsic (rewards, salary and other compensation) and intrinsic (recognition, promotion, other esteem-related feedback).

2. Employees work toward work-related goals based upon their perceived value of these goals balanced against the effort required to achieve these goals. Just because the organization has set an appropriate work goal doesn't mean that the individual will work toward the goal. The individual needs to accept the goal as worthy of their effort before they will work toward the goal.
3. Employees will work harder for a high-level goal if they are given feedback on their progress and can envision their achievement of this goal.
4. Employees seek the high-order needs of competence and self-determination (ability to determine their own course of action).
5. Individuals are not motivated to work toward organizational goals unless these goals can be accepted as an individual goal.
6. Employees that are given feedback concerning their performance toward a goal will continue or adapt their behavior toward the goal (maintain their effort toward the goal) or will change their perception of the value of the goal (to justify their effort and progress toward the goal).
7. In or out of the work environment, people identify goals, begin working toward the goals while observing and evaluating their progress toward the goal, and formulate a response toward the goal (which can be to put less or more effort toward the goal).

8. The evaluated progress toward an accepted goal results in self- and work satisfaction and a sense of pride and feelings of achievement.
9. People perceive higher personal satisfaction from work when their roles possess the following attributes: personal significance, variety, feedback, responsibility, autonomy and identification with the result of the work.

With the above processes in mind you may have a better opportunity to influence the individual and group behaviors within the groups that you will need to manage. If you are going to establish hard-to-reach goals for the group members they need to be able receive feedback toward these goals. Positive feedback is more motivating than negative feedback, but negative feedback is better than none.

Positive Attitude

All motivation comes from inside you—intrinsic motivation. External rewards can provide goals that you perceive to have valuable consequences and that you can be motivated to work for, but your motivation is still driven by your desire for the perceived consequences of your efforts. Whether or not you work toward a goal is based upon your perception of the goals. If you choose to perceive of a goal as worthy of being attained (and believe you can attain it) you will work toward the goal, measuring your progress and continually reevaluating your progress against the effort that you put forth, and correcting your efforts.

You can choose your attitude as well. If you are motivated toward a goal of advancement within the organization, your performance will be related to the energy and enthusiasm that you bring to your work. Your relationships within the organization and with your clients will be impacted by the attitude and drive that you exhibit. Attitude is contagious, and your positive attitude toward work and your goals will trigger a positive attitude in the others within the organization.

Additionally, your role as Project Manager also makes you the cheerleader for the successful achievement of your group's goals. In a sense a leader helps the followers see the value of their efforts toward the group's goals. The delivery of the project in accordance with the project plan, budget and schedule will certainly help the individuals within your team achieve their individual goals within the organization. Beyond that, however, the inspiration of the team members for high-performance and sensitivity to others and the client will allow the project to go from a good project to a great one. Beyond coordinating the team member's efforts toward the successful completion of the deliverable, you need to motivate them to achieve their personal goals in the process and be growing within the organization in order to achieve their own success.

Finally, with respect to your own personal attitude, I like the saying "You can't choose what happens to you, but you can choose your response." I realize that I have not always responded to frustrating situations in a way that I am proud of, but I am continually evaluating and working toward improving my response.

Mentoring

Just as people spent time with you showing you 'the ropes' and helping you understand the technical aspects of your job, you can help your team members understand how to be successful in their own career growth. As an established and experienced professional you have the opportunity to share your earlier experiences. Really, all this takes is time. Take the time to pull some of your team members aside and spend some time with them. Have them ask for advice and input from you concerning your own career path and perspectives. Because you are freshly through the process your input might be more valid to them than someone from higher in the management team.

17 EMOTIONAL INTELLIGENCE

Emotional Intelligence is a concept popularized by Daniel Goleman in the 1990s and relates to a person's ability to be aware of and work with the emotional content of their information processing processes. Because of the makeup of our minds, we process emotions at the same time and with many of the same cognitive resources as we process data. Because of this, the processing of emotions can slow down or block the cognitive evaluation of the situation. On the positive side, the processing of emotional data helps us recall information and events, which can help us process and store important aspects and events of our lives.

On a sub-conscious level, emotions operate at the level of sensations, awareness and alertness which can rise to the conscious level in the form of arousal. At some level, a person can learn to tune into and be aware of some of these emotional stimuli. At the conscious level we can begin to understand and respond to these stimuli, and even control them. Many of these emotions are learned stimulus patterns, and relate to how we value different options, and thus are largely socially influenced. The affect our mood and perspectives, and thus influence our thinking and decision making. The important aspect of this is that they are *learned behaviors*.

Emotions can be good and used to positive effect. I don't believe that anyone would like to go through life while blocking out the emotions of empathy, joy, love or peacefulness. They are useful in our daily lives and in making the right decisions about our future activities and how we apply our energies. People learn to experience and value emotions through physiological and social development, often following social cues about the appropriate response to a situation. Male and female responses to common cues are significantly different due to their different sexual and social development and gender perspectives.

These emotions provide the 'value' that the brain places on information, and which helps you to organize the information. During emotional or stressful times, however, it can negatively affect our processing of information or our decision making processes. Negative emotional information which overdrives the cognitive processes, is called emotional flooding, and drives the attention toward the physiological responses to the immediate situation. Therefore, just as emotions help provide the 'drive' to go after things that we desire, these same emotional tags can disrupt our processing and decision making.

Long-term emotional responses are moods—and are triggered by the general way that we look at the world. If we look at the world in an optimistic manner we have a positive mental attitude with all the healthy attributes associated with a positive outlook. If we are pessimistic we have a bad mood which can lead to stress and the physiological responses which arise therefrom. Under stressful conditions you are more open to influence from others, and stress limits your creativity and ability to explore new behaviors and responses. Stress and the associated presence of adrenaline puts the body in a defensive mode, not open to contemplation but to action. Responses in stressful situations will go to tried and true methods of problem resolution as opposed to creative thinking and new solutions. You need to be comfortable and out of stressful situations in order to be able to think creatively. Have you ever noticed that you have new and creative thoughts about work opportunities when you are on vacation?

That being said, there is a minimal level of stress which is helpful to get people energized and for enhanced learning.

Emotional Intelligence

Our emotions then control aspects of our behavior from our decision making to our moods. Thus it seems logical that it would be important to be aware of, understand and properly deal with our emotional states. Emotional intelligence is the ability to understand and respond appropriately to our emotional states and their resultant effects on our cognitive processing and behavior. Emotional intelligence has several components which we will review individually: self-awareness and self-management.

Self-awareness

Obviously, self-awareness has to do with our awareness of our emotional states, and how they affect our thinking processes, behavior and performance. If we know that we are prone to anger or quick responses we can begin to flag our emotions as they begin to affect us and maneuver for an appropriate response.

The first step in managing self-awareness is becoming aware of your emotions. It begins with the awareness that we all process emotional content at the same time that we process the information that we bring in from the world. This emotional content comes from our previous experiences and through social learning from the groups that we belong to. This emotional content affects our perspectives and thought processes. This can be good in that the 'gut sense' from our real-world experience is esteemed to be very valuable in problem identification and selecting the correct solution to a known and repeatable problem. Businesses hold the ability to read and understand market changes and make proper responsive decisions in high esteem.

This same ability to evaluate information, see trends and create responses based upon past experiences can also be detrimental. In times of industry or environmental change, the solutions that worked in the past may not be appropriate in the future. Applying yesterday's solutions to tomorrow's problems could avoid the real solution to what is perceived as a traditional problem and may put your organization at a significant disadvantage, having not taken advantage of a first-mover opportunity in the industry.

For this reason, you need to be aware of the emotional content of your information processing. Your previous experiences, especially the successful and non-successful experiences, provide your bias or cloud your information gathering and processing. If you are aware of the emotional 'weighting' that is being applied to the information you are evaluating you have a better ability to make more effective decisions. You should also be acutely aware of the role of environmental change in your information gathering—are the situations and experiences that you have had in the past going to help solve the problems going forward?

A second significant component to self-awareness is accurately assessing your own strengths and limitations. Because of our ego it is very difficult for us to properly evaluate our own personal skill sets. This is where we need to seek and process feedback on our performance and get honest input from others, evaluating and properly weighing the information about ourselves.

This is a particularly difficult aspect of self-evaluation and self-improvement. Getting someone to assist you in gathering, sorting and providing accurate, factual information about your performance is vital to your growth and development. How do you sense and relate to people? Are you an emotional person and how do these emotions play into your relationships with others? How are you perceived by others? What are your preferences associated with working with others? Are you empathetic? Do you have a sense for the organization and the feelings and attitudes within the organization? These are all areas where you need to understand how your attitudes and feelings affect your performance and how people perceive you. This is difficult information to gather, sort and interpret in a logical manner.

It should be noted that individuals vary in their ability to receive and accurately process information about themselves. It is difficult to step out of our body (and ego) and realistically look at ourselves, our strengths and our behaviors. This inability to realistically process information about ourselves could create a ceiling through which we will not be able to advance. Because we have created strategies and preferences for dealing with people, situations and frustrated progress, these developed strategies may be effective or may need to be improved over time. One of the biggest challenges to be overcome is the ability to receive, process, and act on information about your personality, preferences and behaviors.

Self-Management

The other day I was traveling to Liberia on a complicated series of connections. I received an automated response from the airlines indicating that the flight had been cancelled. When I was able to get an agent I was only able to determine that the flight had been cancelled and I was re-booked for two days later. Several hours later I was talking to an agent again and found out that only my flight from Atlanta to JFK was cancelled. If I could have dug that information out in the heat of the moment, I could have made alternate plans to drive to an alternate airport and hop on a shuttle to JFK. Because I did not think clearly at the moment, and was processing my emotions, I was blocked from thinking about other viable options.

Self-management deals with these emotional responses once they have been engaged. It begins with the recognition of our emotional state, an understanding of our own programmed pre-disposition to certain thoughts and a deliberate response to mitigate this thought if it is deemed inappropriate. This process is also known as self-control, and is especially appropriate in the face of an emotional or frustrating situation. But because we are continually processing information and emotional content, we need to be aware of the emotional bias present in all of our evaluative situations.

Because our biases and programmed responses are learned behaviors, there are steps that we can begin to take to in order to develop better identification and control mechanisms for our processes and responses. These include:

- Soliciting feedback. Most people receive little *effective* feedback and virtually none associated with the negative aspects of their responses and perspectives. You should solicit honest feedback from someone that you trust to expose your 'warts' and help you get to the bottom of your

biased perspectives and emotional response pre-disposition.
- Identify a coach to help you be aware of and develop a positive response to your high-stress situations. One way to begin to get beyond the immediate situation is to envision a future state where you are beyond the current crisis and envision the response to the decisions that you are contemplating now. Some management selection processes include placement into a high-stress scenario to see how the applicant will respond.
- Put yourself in the 'line of fire'. Accompany others within the organization and watch how they handle stressful or problematic situations. Learning about being in a stressful situation when you are in a low-risk situation allows you to witness and understand what the high-stress situation is like and in the future you will be more prepared for the situation. If you have the chance to see what emotional flooding looks and/or feels like could be an important learning opportunity. The important thing to keep in mind is that this is a temporary situation, and once you see these situations and know that the outcomes are

reasonable and less threatening they won't have the emotional impact that they did.
- Separate yourself from the stressful situations when you are trying to figure out a proper response or solution. This will allow you to begin to focus on alternative, peaceful situations which will allow you to reset your emotional state. Try to avoid significant responses while you are emotionally flooded or under a stressful pressure.
- Get additional input on any decisions that you need to make under stressful conditions. Have other people ask independent questions which will get you processing all of the available information and not just your emotional content.
- Show empathy and truthfulness in your feelings—be genuine. People will trust you if they deal with the same individual and responses consistently—this will provide them with a sense of your integrity.

Appropriate responses all begin with your sensitivity to your own feelings and emotions and how they play into your daily decisions. When things happen to frustrate you, how do you respond? Remember—you can't always control the situation; you can only control your response to the situation.

Achievement Orientation

Your peers, co-workers your friends and members of your family are continually picking up on your motivation and energy. The energy that you bring to your work relationship is important to your success in the same way that your energy and presence contributes to the other relationships in your life. People interpret the energy and drive that you bring to your relationships to reflect the importance of these relationships and activities have to you.

Your achievement orientation reflects the energy and drive that you contribute toward being successful in your organization. At the various levels of your development, this drive may focus on obtaining skills and honing capabilities that vary, but the energy with which you pursue personal improvement and skill enhancement reflects on the capabilities that you will have and the opportunities that will be available within (and potentially outside of) the organization.

It is surprising to me how many good technical people are plugging along in their jobs, perhaps waiting on a new opportunity to land in their lap. Good leaders are always looking for fresh talent and want to help potential rising stars to be successful. The drive toward acquiring new skills is easily recognized and sets the stage for future growth opportunities.

This drive should reflect your own personal standards and be genuine, not just a set of activities being exhibited to encourage advancement. These should reflect your personal nature, optimism, initiative and drive for excellence within your work and personal life.

Impact on Team Dynamics

When you are managing teams, you need to be even more cognizant of your emotions and responses. When working with teams from an emotional perspective, realize that there is a distinct difference between new and experienced teams. New teams are forming, trying to figure out how they want to work together and working to establish norms, working relationships, and culture. They are trying to establish behavior patterns and ways of getting along and understanding their collective goals and environment. These groups are pliable, and introducing new ideas and concepts are usually met with an open mind.

Experienced teams, like organizations, have unique and pre-set behavior patterns that have been socially negotiated and create behavior expectations within and among them. New teams may be forming these patterns, working with each other and determining what is allowed, encouraged and forbidden. You can help groups establish healthy work patterns by encouraging positive behaviors and the correct interpretation of social cues.

Within the capabilities of the group, you can help them understand and properly conceptualize the roles that they are playing and the goals of the group. If they can understand the group function, dynamics and challenges they can better put their behavior (and the behavior of others) into proper context.

This concludes the section on the identification and attributes and skills related to emotional intelligence as it relates to the professional development portion of your career track. Many of these skills can be utilized at your current developmental level and some are forward looking. As you have opportunity to advance in organizational management there will be higher expectations about your emotional processing, evaluation, understanding and control.

18 LEADERSHIP SKILLS

First, it is important to note that I intended for the Leadership Skills section to follow the section on Emotional intelligence. At the fundamental level, many of these leadership skills have their foundation in the ability to understand and control the emotional processes and their contribution to people's behaviors and attitudes. I believe it is very difficult for an emotionally immature person to achieve a significant position of leadership. In order to respect and follow a leader, people need to be able to see maturity and consistency in the leader's behaviors and thus his/her intentions.

In this section you will become aware of traits that you need to internalize and work with and eventually to embed into your psyche. These sound like high-level concepts, but if you maintain them in the top of your mind you can continue to go back to them and reinforce them. As you see yourself beginning to compromise in these areas you can challenge yourself to stay close to your espoused values, maintaining your integrity (developing and reinforcing your moral principles).

At this time you are in the character-building portion of your career. As you begin to deal with your peers within the organization in order to get project outcomes completed and deal in professional ways with customers, you will need to have established and be cultivating an honest and upstanding reputation. In this section we will begin to look at the attributes that you should consider building into your own personal character. These characteristics would become the foundation for your reputation and would pave the road for future leadership opportunities. These attributes should be developed into your everyday activities, behaviors and relationships.

Trustworthy and Reliable. It may go without saying, but a trusting relationship must underlie all of your relationships. People must know that they are dealing with a genuine person, who will be truthful in their dealings and when you give your word they can count on it. As you begin to have employees work on your team you they need to be able to trust you. Hopefully they will recall the times when you were delivering the technical aspects of the products and services and that you acted with integrity and punctuality. If they saw you working hard and were successful they will be able to see an advancement path for themselves.

In the future, this trust will play an important part of your leadership characteristics. The people that would be working with you as their leader will need to know that you are being honest and upstanding. They will need comfort that the goals that you put forth are worthy of their effort and that they will benefit from the achievement of these goals. This relationship can be real or can be imagined by the followers; however they are expending effort toward the goals based upon their individual motivation. Most theories of motivation (which is considered a sustained effort toward a goal) have some component of belief in a reward or positive outcome for achieving a goal. Followers that are performing work and putting forth efforts toward a leader's goals have some expectation that it will achieve their own personal goals, either real or imagined, which have been communicated (or implied) by the leader.

The bottom line is—if you want people to trust you in the future, you need to lay the foundation when you are working on a professional level. This should never be compromised.

Respect for others. You need to have respect for the other employees within the organization 100% of the time. If they are employed by the organization they are contributing to the common goals that you are working for. Whether you believe their performance can be improved or they are doing the best that they can, they deserve the respect for the efforts they are putting forth. You may not agree with their personal lifestyle, belief system or the way that they treat others, but there are formal channels for questioning their behaviors in these areas (if it is appropriate).

If you are in a position of supervision of a person with personality issues, you should consult the Human Resources director for guidance as to how (and whether) you should approach the situation. If it relates to the performance of their job or the effectiveness of their work they could be coached or the information could be presented in a more formal way.

Gossip can be defined as idle talk or rumor

about the personal or private affairs of others. As I have said before, this is very damaging, both to the person being talked about and the person sharing this information. Under most circumstances, people just don't trust others who share gossip and innuendo. Whether substantiated or not, people know that if you will share information about others, what is to stop you from sharing information about them? Remember—you are building a foundation for long-term relationships with others. Do not risk that relationship by sharing stories, no matter how appealing you find it at the time.

Honesty and Integrity. Closely allied to trust, honesty is the attribute by which people know that you are sincere and truthful. When people deal with you in the future they need to know that they are dealing with your genuine thoughts and feelings.

The people that I know that I don't believe are sincere are a great disappointment to me. I always feel like I am talking to the programmed response that they are putting forth and not to the real person. Whatever they are truly feeling is hidden behind the façade. I have been truly put off by the feeling that the person was not being genuine with me, and to this day I am courteous but do not engage with people that I do not feel are honest or genuine with me.

It can be easy to be read as insincere, though, in our daily lives. Being honest and present with people takes time, and often time is balanced with production in a workplace environment. Perhaps finding some private time outside of the work environment (lunch) would provide a good opportunity to get to know the others that you work with personally. Once you know about their home situation, value system and where they come from it is a lot easier to get beyond the little nuances that you may find different and questionable from time to time. They also get to see that you are real and interested in them and their success.

Empathy and approachability. In a similar vein, empathy implies that you understand and share the feelings of those individuals that you value in the workplace. Again, this needs to be genuine and come from the heart. For many of the employees at work, they likely spend more time at work than they are able to spend with their families. Their relationships at work are important to them and as such they should be important to you.

You should be open to connection and conversation as your work will allow. I understand that work requirements constrain your time, and there is life outside of work. You should, however, let people know that if you are not available to spend time with them at a particular time that you will try to be available to them in the future. People will appreciate and remember the personal time that you spent with them, especially if you took time from your personal time to do so.

Also—be yourself! It is extremely important for you to be genuine, be authentic. People will appreciate getting to know you and grow with you. If you have questions or concerns you need to ask them in a friendly and sincere way, but your co-workers need to see your value systems at work in the ways that you work and live.

Achievement Orientation. I have also mentioned this attribute in the past, so I won't dwell on it except to say that if you want to aspire to be a manager or leader in the organization someday, your peers they need to see that you are committed to personal excellence and achievement. They also need to see that your goals and working ethics are in harmony with the strivings of the organization.

Respect for others. This is showing admiration for someone based upon their abilities or other qualities or achievements. Respect is a very subjective attribute, and varies depending upon the perspective and values of the organizational members. For the humble person, however, it doesn't cost anything to give it away.

Self-control and Work-Life Balance. For a moment I want to talk to you about your life. There is a constant tension between becoming successful at work and having a successful life and quality relationships at home. You will need to find your own balance around having a successful career, climbing the corporate ladder and, potentially, organizational leadership on one hand and having a successful life, family and relationships at home. In an age of multiple breadwinners in a household, this is truly a tension to the home relationship and requires balance and good communication.

I would encourage you to establish goals and lines in the sand on both sides, and establish relationships where these lines are respected. On both sides there will be give and take periodically, but having established a balanced relationship allows those periodic variances to occur without causing a major problem. It should be noted that you don't see too many tombstones saying "He wishes that he spent more time at work."

Finally, consider your health. Stress is a significant factor in the modern work life, and the remedy to stress is relaxation, a realistic perspective and moderate exercise. Develop a schedule for your life which respects your exercise and rest cycles. Find a space and time for you to be able to unwind appropriately and properly.

Alcohol should be used in moderation. Tobacco provides more energy for work but comes with huge addicting and health side-effects. Other drugs have no place in a professional life. Your body is the vessel that allows your brain to carry out the rest of the things in this book. If you do not properly maintain the body, the rest of what I'm telling you really doesn't matter—you won't be around to enjoy the fruits of your labor.

It's all about self-control. Who controls your mind and body?

Management Skills

19 UNDERSTANDING THE ORGANIZATION

If you have been successful in your technical development and have demonstrated competency in your professional skills, you may be asked to assume some management responsibilities. Especially in a smaller organization, people are often asked to take on multiple roles or additional responsibility.

If you are asked to assume some management responsibilities it is helpful to have some insight into how a business works, the various functions of a business, and how they fit together. This high level insight allows you to understand your new roles and responsibilities in the context of the larger environment.

Please keep in mind that this is just my perspective of a very high-level overview of the business organization, how it functions and how its parts relate to each other. There are degrees and careers devoted to studying the business. I will, however, try to set the business world in a professional context for you.

Business Overview

So what is a business? I earlier identified an organization as a group of people who get together in order to achieve a particular purpose or goal. A business is a special type of an organization which is dedicated to its mission and funds its growth through the generation of profits (income in excess of its costs to do business). Business organizations have a special standing in the United States—they are essentially given the same rights as a human being—the ability to borrow money, own property, hire and fire people and to engage in commerce. As a part of this relationship, the corporate structure shields the shareholders and directors from much of the organization's liability.

There are different ways of organizing a business, but the most popular type for a smaller business is a Limited Liability Company or as a Corporation for a larger organization. The advantage that a business which is organized as an LLC or a corporation has is that the members of the board of directors, which drives the activities of the corporation, are isolated from liability for most of the actions of corporation.

Once we identify, select and join a business organization it becomes important to our life. Each organization has a unique perspective which is embedded in its mission and goals. Each organization also has a culture, or set of values and behaviors that new entrants need to learn and accommodate or at least assimilate into.

Businesses allow us to specialize in a particular area that interests us, and allows us to develop and maintain an in-depth knowledge and capability in our chosen area. Businesses attract individuals with (or contracts for services with others that have) skills in all of the business divisions below which allow for a full complement of services and capabilities within the organization.

Business Divisions

Some businesses are larger and have multiple divisions with the organization and other businesses are small and share the responsibilities for these activities among its employees. The main divisions or activities that each business has, at least at some level, are as follows:

Marketing. Marketing works to develop a public image or 'brand' for the organization. This brand, like we discussed for the individual, allows the business to differentiate itself in its market—the business sector that it operates in. Is the business a boutique, specialist or participate in the discount market? The goal of a marketing group is to make its competencies and specialties known to its target market—to attract attention to the organization.

Because people are very busy and have limited available attention, they goal of the marketing efforts will be to tell the story by creating compelling narratives and having attractive attributes. Once people's attention is gained the target should be attracted to the organization, the celebrated individuals and the activity which is being celebrated. If a personal connection can be developed the program will be better remembered and celebrated by the potential client.

A marketing department (or the people within the company who are responsible for marketing) will be monitoring the market segment in which the company participates. By constantly analyzing the market and understanding the company's position they can help guide the organization to best position itself to thrive and perhaps grow.

The marketing department will be interested in knowing how the company is thought about in the industry? Do the company's clients (and potential clients) understand the benefits that the company has to offer? Do they understand the current capabilities of the company and the advantages that the company offers?

Companies usually differentiate themselves through the value of their provided services. Are they an inexpensive option, do they provide a high quality of service, or provide a good value (mix of quality product and value).

Professional service organizations are unique in their offerings—the value of these services are often directly related to the processes that the organizations have, the persons delivering the services and the experiences of the group. For professional service, the customer's experience is ultimately driven by or moderated by the experience and personality of the individual providing the services or at point with the client.

Another goal of the marketing group is to qualify the clients. They will submit information to potential clients but will also evaluate them based upon their potential value as a client. Will these clients appreciate the value that our organization provides or will they make future purchasing decisions based upon pricing or other subjective evaluation which may not promote long-term relationships?

When presenting information to the client the marketing group will focus on framing the information (and the organization) in a positive way. This will happen through the emphasis of information which focuses on the organization's strengths and de-emphasize those aspects of the organization which may be detrimental to the organization's perception. Sometimes a little controversy helps to emphasize the positive aspects of the organization's positions, especially if they are altruistic and have high social content.

Finally, the marketing group is interested in reinforcing a positive reputation in the market. They may be able to facilitate the conversations about the positive aspects of the organization, but ultimately the company's reputation is built over time as they complete projects, deliver services and satisfy (or don't satisfy) customers. Ultimately, some people, as they are able, will pay a premium price to work with a company (or the attendant representatives) which has a good reputation. Building a good reputation takes time and requires everyone in the organization delivering consistent and excellent services—the best type of marketing you can have.

Sales. The marketing department is responsible for helping build a positive environment for the business and to establish the 'brand', but that doesn't directly bring revenues to the organization. Actually transacting for delivering goods or services to a client in exchange for consideration (usually money) is called *sales*. Without the sales transaction there would be no revenues and no business.

All service transactions and the sales of

many goods rely on the client's trust in the organization. The client needs something to happen—a service that they need for their ongoing operations or a component, materials or equipment to perform some function in their operations. They are relying on the goods or services provided by your organization to be delivered in accordance with your 'promise'. In the case of a service, they are relying on your previous transactions or the relationships of others that they trust.

A warranty can help bring comfort that the component will perform as expected or will provide a guaranteed performance over some limited timeframe. For many products the warranty or performance guarantee has become a standard feature of the components, and can be extended by the client, shifting the risk for a longer-term performance guarantee to the manufacturer (or a third party) for a fee (which is technically called 'risk reversal').

It is important to keep in mind that you are not selling your package of goods and services, but you are selling the capability to solve a problem for the client for fill a client's needs. As I have said, I have had clients in the past whose favorite saying was "Make my problems go away." It was my favorite saying, too.

Thus, if you are an accountant you are not selling your staff's time, you are providing insight and proper documentation and information about your client's operations that are required for government submission and data for the proper operation of their business. If you are an architect you are not selling time or your capabilities, you are helping a client take their ideas and needs and delivering a facility that will meet those needs in a way that they could not do themselves.

Building on this concept, the successful sales of a business' services is listening to and accurately identifying your client's needs. You can then utilize your own staff (and perhaps other support people, called sub-contractors or sub-consultants) to meet these needs. Meeting these needs and giving your client a good experience during the project delivery allows a deeper relationship with the client.

By listening to the client you can understand what the client values. What is important to the client, and how can you provide services that are in alignment with these values? Clients and customers are not all made the same, and unless you listen to them you will apply your standard package to their custom needs and desires. If you correctly identify the types and components of services that they desire you will be able to customize your service delivery to target their needs. The additional effort that you may have taken to give them the other 'standard' components that they don't want can be expended to exceed their expectations in the areas they desire. The process of listening to and quantifying the client's desires allows you to be more focused in service delivery, deliver excellent value and instill customer confidence in the efforts you are putting forth to them. It also helps you frame your sales proposal to their exact needs.

While you are having deep communications

with your client, take the time to educate your client about their needs and how your services are designed to deliver value based upon those needs. This helps establish trust and shows your intention to truly help the client identify and accurately articulate their needs and make good business decisions about their investment in problem solutions. It also helps you align their and your expectations so that the delivered project will satisfy them.

Finance and Accounting. These groups deal with collecting and processing the financial performance of the organization. Accounting is concerned with collecting and organizing the information about the costs and revenues of the organization and presents this information in ways that organizations can use for effective management and financial reporting. Finance is the science (art?) of watching the money entering and leaving a business and managing access to financial resources and its allocation.

Accounting information is collected and presented in standardized formats which allows the organization to look at its profitability (Profit and Loss Statements) on a monthly (or periodic) basis, longer-term profitability and asset tracking (Balance Sheet) and the ability of the organization to generate cash and grow or continue operations (Cash Flow Statements). Each of these statements have associated metrics and ratios which allow individuals managing the company from within and monitoring the company from outside the organization to track the relative health of the organization the same way doctors track attributes of your blood during a periodic checkup and recommend future actions based upon these values.

Companies track their production costs (variable costs) and fixed overhead costs in order to determine what to charge for their services and to anticipate their profitability. Company profits allow for compensation (and hence the retention) of its key players, provides revenues for company growth, and provides a buffer against lean economic periods. Healthy companies have a varied baseload of long-term clients where they can provide high-value services and receive high returns. If your company provides a valuable service to a client (and helps them generate a significant amount of revenues or save them significant costs) then your company's services are worth a premium price, regardless of the cost of the services—this is the foundation of value-based pricing.

Thus the accounting group provides the controls systems which allows for the efficient operation of the organization. The Finance group allows the organization to finance and manage the organization's cash requirements. Organizations require cash to purchase equipment, pay their workers, acquire critical services and procure raw materials, among other vital requirements. These services require cash to be available at certain times to allow for the payments when they are due. The cash ideally comes from completed orders or services but can come through bank loans or other operating loans as may be appropriate.

Companies can use various techniques to

access cash, including selling stock, selling bonds, taking out loans for equipment or establishing lines of credit with financial institutions to accommodate short-term needs. All of these forms of financing are appropriate for different financial circumstances and all allow the company to access financing in an appropriate manner for their operations.

Production or Service Delivery: every profitable organization delivers something 'valuable' to its client. *Production* usually refers to the ongoing (and usually repeating) processes which deliver a product to a client. This production can include procurement, receipt of raw materials, assembly, testing, packaging and shipping for a manufactured product. There are as many processes and variations associated with the production process as there are varied products on the market, however an organization's 'process flow' allows for the understanding of the production operations. Companies try to make their production processes as efficient as possible, while still maintaining the quality of the finished product.

Service delivery is unique to every market and provider-client relationship. Often services are provided on an individual or project-related basis. Because of this the perceived quality of the provided services varies significantly with the particular exchange (project), individuals that are participating in the exchange and their ability to communicate effectively.

Quality is the characteristic of the product or service which allows it to meet the needs and expectations of the client. When your organization contracts with a client it agrees to provide a product or service which meets the needs of the client, and that is usually a requirement of these contracts. If the product or service meets these requirements 100% of the time it is considered to be of high quality. Different clients have different types and level of quality that they require or desire.

The *value* is the subjective measure of the perceived qualities of the product or service per unit of cost. Everyone values different characteristics of a product or service according to their own perceived value system and desires. For example, do you drive a Kia or a BMW? Organizations attempt to quantify these values through a procurement process, and allow for measuring the relative value of the offerings from various vendors.

An important aspect of delivering valuable services to your clients is to listen to them. What aspects of the provided products and services do they value? What is important to them? More importantly, what aspects of your provided services are they not interested in paying for? It is appropriate to sit down with your client's representative and ask them what aspects of their services do they appreciate and really like, and which ones would they rather not have (and thus not pay for). If you can fine-tune your product offerings to your clients you will have a higher probability of developing a good long-term relationship with them. As clients and their needs and desires change periodically, it is helpful to keep the channels of communication open to assure that your company is providing the types and levels of services desired at the appropriate pricing.

Maintenance is the group responsible for maintaining ongoing production equipment operating in accordance with the company's requirements to assure the quality of the finished product. If the production operations can be conceptualized as a 'machine' then it is easy to conceive that the machine will wear, require periodic maintenance and adjustment. Groups that are familiar with these processes can learn to optimize the operations, delivering high reliability of the equipment and high quality of the finished products. Usually standardizing on products and maintenance processes will help the efficiency of the group.

Preventative maintenance is the processes whereby failures in the system are anticipated and the production equipment is adjusted and components serviced and replaced in advance of their failure. This reduces the probability of an equipment failure during a production run, which can cause interruption and delays to the production process or affect the quality of the finished product. Preventative Maintenance, or PM, usually involves the statistical tracking of component failure, adjustment and wear on the production components and strategic replacement and adjustment to allow for efficient and high-quality operations.

Known variously as *Human Resources* or *Human Relations* (HR), this group has the responsibility for managing the relationships among the organization and the individuals and for complying with the local and federal regulations associated with the workplace. Because humans are the ones that perform all of the valued services within an organization, the acquisition and retention of good employees is vital to an organization's success. To fulfill this need, the HR group participates in needs identification, recruitment, assessment, acquisition, compensation, education, correction and dismissal of employees as well as compliance with a myriad of regulations associated with the employment relationship.

Beginning in the early industrial era, employers began to offer other benefits to their employees in order to attract and retain high performing workers. As time went on, many of these benefits (retirement, health care, vacation plans, vehicles, etc.) have become institutionalized into our organizations and have become standard compensation package offerings. Additionally, regulations have been developed which require the provision of some of these services as a part of the compensation packages for full-time employees (family leave provisions, Social Security retirement packages, health care) and others have specific legal requirements (tax-protected retirement funds).

The modern professional employee is attracted and retained by a complicated mix of required and voluntary programs which includes salary and incentive programs, and which are managed by the HR department. This department also manages the collective expectations of groups of employees, managing perceived pay-for-work equity, and collective benefit requirements. Managing the details of the employee's benefit packages has become an important aspect of the HR department.

The *Purchasing* department provides for the acquisition of raw materials and equipment for production as well as other services which may be needed to deliver the services to the client. This usually includes the labor which is not being performed by the provider's own human resources (employees). This additional labor may include sub-contractors, consultants and other specialty services as may be required periodically in order to complete a particular project or provide a specific service.

The purchasing group manages the procurement process through a group of standardized processes, often including processes which are standardized within a particular industry sector. By standardizing on processes such as RFP (request for proposal), RFQ (request for quote) and standard-language contract agreements the purchasing group can standardize the delivery of products and services and minimize the variation in pricing and service delivery.

Legal departments are comprised of (or are contracted with) attorneys who are familiar with business-related legal issues and provide the standard contracts and forms of relationships between and among organizations. They are also involved in interpreting specific contracts and complex procurement and production relationships throughout the organization and within the regulatory environment.

Risk-management. Because catastrophic issues can devastate an organization, most organizations have insurance which will provide management against risk and assist the organization deal with significant problems. Many organizations have other risk management groups, such as a safety department and quality-control program which, in their own way, each attempt to identify risks proactively and take steps to mitigate the frequency and significance of problems.

Management is generally referred to as those individuals who provide the oversight and direction to the organization. Different types of organizations have widely-varied structures for organizing the responsibilities and communication within organizations, but the organizing themes are usually oriented around an organizational chart. At the top is usually a Board of Directors which provides the high-level guidance and important strategic decisions and direct the overall direction of the organization.

In larger organizations the Chief Executive Officer (CEO) is responsible for executing the company's program in accordance with the Board's plan. The CEO directs the activities through his/her other officers, Chief Financial Officer (CFO), Chief Information Officer (CIO) and other directors which are often collectively referred to as 'C-level' management.

In smaller organizations you often have a company President who is the chief administrative officer and answerable to the Board. The President may have Vice Presidents with responsibilities for various divisions (or sub-divisions) of the organization and Managers below them to provide management for the specific activities of their group. Usually organizations are organized by discipline which allows for the processes within the various groups to be optimized.

Organizations which provide much of their services through Project Management processes often are organized by technical disciplines as 'silos' with projects represented by horizontal groups which are organized of members from each of these silos on their project teams. These teams form in order to provide a specific project or deliverable and then are dismissed to form into a different team. An organization represented by technical silos and multiple horizontal projects is considered a 'matrix organization.'

Business and Market Processes

Organizations, as we have discussed, involve people organizing together to accomplish a goal which utilizes the specialized talents of the individuals and provides products or services to clients based upon their needs. Businesses in various stages of their development have unique needs and see their competitive market differently. New businesses are in the process of learning about and probing the market, identifying valuable clients and understanding their needs. Initially they will be focused on establishing credibility within their industry and developing experience for higher and more valuable opportunities.

Older businesses are established in the market and understand the market and its drivers. They have production resources which are geared for the market as it currently exists and understands the world in accordance with these production and delivery standards. This momentum gives them a perspective about market changes that are shifts and trends in the market that follow these traditional patterns, but may not recognize disruptive shifts in the industry which introduces new technologies and shifts the ways that the traditional industry operates.

Because businesses are essentially an artificial and legal 'individual' with rights and privileges to transact business on behalf of the owners under the direction of the board, it is helpful to conceptualize the business as having other individual traits. Like individuals, organizations learn about their markets and develop their capabilities from its peers and customers and from previous experiences. When they are successful organizations repeat their successes and when they are not they learn behaviors that they will try not to replicate. That is why new technologies and other disruptive shifts in industries are more easily identified and readily responded to by new companies that are not locked into traditional mindsets and can more easily conceptualize thinking outside of these traditional themes.

Company Valuations

A valuation is the process of estimating the relative value of the company. Using the stock market, investor groups evaluate the relative value of the company and their earning potential every day based upon news and trends in the business environment. In a similar manner, all of a company's value is eventually tied to its ability to provide goods and services and generate profit, either now or in the future.

The traditional earnings-based valuation is based upon an estimation of the profitability of the corporation in the future. Based upon the earnings (usually over the past 5 years) weighted inversely by the number of years back, an annualized earnings amount can be generated. This earning value per year can then be used to estimate the annual earnings going forward. This annualized earning can be projected for a number of years and discounted based upon industry factors. These discount factors could include the history and quality of clients, stability of the industry and the quality and stability of the primary client contacts. This discount factor also includes factors which comprise the relative risk of the company's profitability (for example, are a majority of the revenues based upon a few important principals or clients or industry relationships that could shift and change the profitability.)

A company's valuation can be viewed in a number of different ways. The price/earnings (P/E) ratio considers the annualized company earnings and compares them with the organization's peers within the industry. If a company has a lower P/E ratio than its peers within an industry it may be a good value. The ultimate goal of a valuation is the estimation of the earning potential of the company (plus the book value of the assets) weighed against the risk associated with the business. The value of the company compares the purchase of a company or some shares of a company with respect to the time-value of money—what else could be done with the money and what the ultimate return on alternate investments might be.

The goal for this section of the book was to introduce basic business concepts on a high-level basis as opposed to a strictly technical perspective. Hopefully it provided an appropriate overview and allowed an introduction to this created entity we call an organization. Some organizations have specific goals that they are focused on achieving, and others have additional goals of generating profits for its investors, which we refer to as businesses.

In the next section we will spend some time talking about how organization' provide value to its clients and how to potentially leverage that value.

20 ADDING VALUE

At a theoretical level, all organizations need to add value to a product or service in order to be viable. Organizations and individuals alike have needs (or wants) that they would like to have satisfied or fulfilled. They would like to have these needs met and often would exchange something of value for the satisfaction of these needs. The more pressing the need and the rarer the satisfaction of these needs are the higher the value that they are willing to offer in exchange for the satisfaction of these needs.

For organizations (and sometimes individuals) the business and regulatory environment is complex, and the specific skills and knowledge to assure compliance with these regulatory requirements and practices may require specialized support from outside the organization as necessary. The increasing levels of specialization and complexity of requirements and solutions may require higher-value services.

Organizations provide services to their customers which they need (or feel that they need). The value of the product or service to the customer is dependent upon several things which are considered 'drivers' for the value of the product.
1. The first is—how important is the service to the client. A small business may not perceive the need for an attorney on a daily

basis, however when an imminent legal issue becomes a threat they are perceived to be very important.
2. A specialized need which requires specialized knowledge or components has a higher value to the client. Because of the inherent nature of this specialization, the value of this offering is inversely proportional to the availability of products or service providers.
3. Timing—having products or services available to clients on an as-needed basis requires a higher cost because slack resources or stocked materials are required to be able to respond on an expedited basis. Customers will pay a premium for the ability to respond to an emergency situation, especially if this is critical to their operations or affects other important stakeholders. Also if there is a timing constraint for the client there may be acceleration costs associated with getting products or services outside of normal production sequences.
4. Competition tends to drive prices to a unified cost floor among different providers. Companies attempt to protect their pricing positions with patents, licensing agreements and branding which gives the appearance of the product being more exclusive or higher quality.

When we consider our organization we often are constrained by the way that we organize our services—that we offer accounting services, engineering services or specific types of products. This is certainly descriptive of our services but does not describe the value that we can provide to our clients. Value can be provided to a client in several different ways. A company can provide a product or service which will save the client money, allow them to do or make something that they can offer at a higher value to their customers, or save them time or effort from their own resources.

If we begin to conceptualize our services in the context of the value that we bring to our clients, we can begin to look at our services as enabling them to do other things. It allows a new lens for evaluating our relationships. An example of this is accounting services—if we consider that our clients do not have to learn how to manage their accounting and are able to pursue other things of higher value, it allows us to look at different ways to accommodate this for the client. It allows us to look at other alternatives that may achieve the same goals for the client.

Organizational Activities

All professional products and services have multiple components associated with the client relationships. These relationships begin with the marketing and sales interactions, establishing relationships with the design and production groups, interaction with accounting departments, management of the project delivery and follow-up services. All of these contact points are opportunities to make the client happy, and contribute to the overall project delivery experience.

Effective organizations manage all of these client contact points (perhaps through a Project Manager or Managing Principal). These contact points and the attending processes within the delivering organization which provide these services reflect the culture of the organization and ability of the employees to work together.

New Technologies

As new technologies are introduced there are several opportunities to support clients. First—new technology platforms are inherently disruptive to the traditional market structure, so as these new technologies are adopted they will provide opportunities for new products into the market. Secondly, as these new technologies are introduced there are support needs to assist companies in the adaptation and implementation of these new technologies. Companies that are proactive in identifying and incorporating these new technologies can provide additional value to their existing clients and perhaps use these technologies to be introduced to new clients.

Communication

Fundamentally, communication is the act of providing and receiving useful information with other people. Communications is a process where information is transmitted from one party, communicated through a medium, and received and interpreted by another. These parties can be individuals, groups or organizations.

Professionals have learned and adopted specific language for their industry. When our customers require specialty services that are outside of their areas of expertise they may need to be educated so that they can request and interpret the services that are being offered. Because they may not understand the language or the special processes that are often present in professional products or services, part of our job is to be the interpreter of information from one group to another.

An excellent example of this is in the area of architectural services. A client may have an idea of what they want—offices, special areas, and a budget amount. They may not consider or understand the amount of parking required, access, types of construction, interior treatments, local zoning and regulations, or scheduling constraints. An architect will take the provided information from the client and produce documents that are specific to the construction trades which allow them to be able to price and build the structure and treatments. The architect will then manage the construction through the bid and construction process, schedule progress and financial releases to the contractor. The architect will then need to manage the expectation of the client and contractor, communicating to each in accordance with the understanding of the norms of procurement and implementation unique to each side.

Thus there is a significant component of communication necessary in each professional relationship. Customers vary significantly in these areas as well. Some may be very savvy about the procurement and use of specialized services while others may not be familiar with the processes and may require a bit of training. It will be important for the professional to assess the knowledge level of the client and be able to communicate with him/her at that level to allow a delivered product/service to be appropriate to their needs and efficiently delivered. Thus, communication is an important aspect of the effectiveness of a professional at delivering their services—providing their 'value'.

Spend the time with your client representative and find out what they value in a consultant relationship. I had a plant engineer tell me that their primary goal was to be able to get home and see their family while his organization was downsizing their staff. He had the financial resources available to procure additional support, and we developed a great working relationship going forward. It wasn't until I spent time understanding his needs that we changed our approach to that relationship.

21 LEVERAGING VALUE

Interesting thing about the 'value' that people put on things—it is completely subjective. During every significant holiday there are lots of advertisements for gold and jewelry. Gold and diamonds, due to their unique qualities, hold lots of intrinsic value. My wife, however, has no interest in jewelry and has been known to refuse to accept jewelry worth thousands of dollars because she has no interest in owning them.

Many brands have that intrinsic value associated with them (BMW, Mercedes, Rolex, etc.) and there is a premium quality about them which allows them to retain this intrinsic value. They hold their value because others are willing to pay a premium price to own them. You can find less expensive transportation and certainly there are much less expensive ways to accurately tell time.

With that in mind, it is up to your organization to be able to learn about your client and determine what is important to them. For some clients, price is the only driver, and these types of clients are not likely to hold high long-term value. These types of clients would not be my highest priority.

Like the products mentioned above, some brands have prestige associated with them, and having a name that is known to your clients may get you in the door. Your reputation is initially seeded through the marketing process and the story you tell. Your organization's reputation is ultimately built, however, by the way people talk about you. Are your customers happy with your services? What do they say about your products or performance to other potential clients? How can you ultimately become the premium brand?

Building a Brand
Your reputation will allow other people to be comfortable beginning to take a risk with your organization initially. The basis of all professional relationships ultimately comes down to trust. Whether you are hiring an attorney or getting a haircut, you have expectations about the outcome of the situation you are about to enter, and the amount of perceived risk of an unexpected (or non-desired outcome) provides tension and stress to the relationship and purchasing decision. If your customer has comfort with the decision that the transaction will have the desired outcome (or at least that the will have the highest probability of a desired outcome) they will have a high satisfaction with the transaction.

The concept of reliability builds on this concept of trust. If your organization consistently delivers products which can be counted upon for long life and high value then the client has comfort with their expectations about future transactions. If your organization has a reputation for reliability and consistency it allows new potential clients to have comfort that their transactions will be satisfactory as well. This predictability is important for developing deep relationships with clients.

The performance/cost ratio is a factor which always exists below the surface. People are consistently evaluating the relative value (performance/cost) of the products and services that they are receiving. Some organizations have processes which drive them to make evaluative decisions periodically, reviewing their purchasing decisions and requiring the users within the organization to re-evaluate the delivered services based upon a provider's peers.

It is certainly appropriate to be aware of what your company's competition is doing so that you can match the services being offered and match industry trends for delivery. Continuous organizational learning, however, focuses on continuously delivering more value. Project and service delivery should be followed up with a lessons learned process—what aspects of the project delivery and client service relationship should and could be improved upon? Once these potential improvements are identified, how can they be internalized into the organization's processes so that the improvement can take place?

One perspective that is helpful in keeping an innovative spirit is to continually ask how your organization could re-define the market. What new products or services in your industry could dramatically change the way people use products (like the example of the i-Phone)? How could our clients receive service and have their needs satisfied differently? What new technologies and strategies could allow new and innovative service-delivery processes?

Scaling
If your organization is essentially a service organization you will have unique challenges with growth—individuals don't scale. Because services are so individualized (or in the terms of projects, very reliant on the individual relationships of the management team) they are difficult to replicate without great care. If your organization primarily delivers services, which are delivered by individuals, you will have two special conditions which will affect your growth. First is, obviously, picking the right people. People are unique bundles of knowledge, skills and abilities, and not all of these will translate into the types of relationships that are valued by your clients. Picking the right people who will mesh with your client's principles and be able to integrate and work effectively is the key to long-term growth and success.

The second is building robust systems within your organization which will direct the organization's activities (and those individuals performing these activities) to consistently and efficiently performing their tasks. These systems should be directing individuals to consistent task performance and workflow consistent with the requirements of the organization. Under most circumstances, rules drive behaviors, which drive habits, and which (usually) ultimately drives perspectives and values. If you want your organization to deal consistently and fairly with your clients your organization's behavior toward its employees needs to model these values.

Personal Value

So here is an interesting concept for you—many of the brand-building concepts described above apply at a fundamental level to your relationship with your employment organization. Your integrity is fundamental to your relationship with the organization—they want to know that they can trust you to act in the best interest of the organization and have an upstanding and positive relationship with the client.

The organization is interested in in knowing that you will be acting consistently with the client and others within the organization. Because an organization's systems were developed in order to allow for a consistent flow, employees with a constant demeanor and predictable behavior will be valued within an organization.

The higher your position within an organization the more important your personal dedication is. With increasing rank the organization is relying more and more upon you to be present and available to make the right decisions for the organization and protect their interests. Depending upon your organization's size, this dedication may be ultimately rewarded by management-level positions and potentially ownership opportunities, or other valued rewards.

Your ability to communicate effectively within the organization, with the client, and eventually with the general public will be an important capability to develop and foster. Many individuals have a challenge with public speaking and organizational leadership. Individuals early in their professional career should volunteer for speaking and volunteer organizational leadership opportunities in order to foster a wider perspective about different organizations and how to effectively communicate with larger groups of people. There are various groups to help individuals learn confidence in public speaking and developing inter-social relationships.

Rewards Systems

Any discussion of the organization's value delivery needs to recognize the role that the reward and compensation system provides to the organization's motivation. Because rewards align the individual's focus and efforts (and theoretically their performance) with those outcomes that the organization values, the organization's reward system is important to employee motivation.

Rewards drive the attraction of new employees to the organization and the retention of these employees. Because replacing an employee is expensive (5 times their monthly salary) the compensation should be designed to retain high value employees. Theoretically, some turnover is healthy for the organization, however, as long as the people leaving are the poorer performers. Therefore, in a reward system the goals should be to retain valuable employees and allow the poor performers to leave. By making the difference in rewards between the high and low performers to be significant the more valuable employees feel satisfied when comparing their rewards with others within and outside of the organization.

Develop reward systems to be based upon the individual's performance. As was said earlier, better performers should receive significantly more rewards than poor performers to motivate individuals toward desired behavior. Managing turnover is essentially managing the anticipated satisfaction of the employees.

In order for these rewards to motivate performance the employees must perceive the rewards to be important to them and they need to be tied in a timely fashion to their effective performance. These rewards can increase skill development if the connection between the desired skills and rewards is clear.

Another important dynamic to consider for reward systems is whether to reward individuals or groups for their performance. Rewarding individuals for their performance and ignoring group performance may trigger feelings of competition within the groups and tension among group participants. In order to develop a good environment for cohesive teaming relationships, groups should be all rewarded for collective successes.

Reward system and culture interact and influence each other. Rewards will drive and reinforce behavior patterns within the organization, which become embedded in and form the organization's culture. Reward administration may create the perception of competition or teamwork within the organization, depending upon how they are created and administered. A reward system can also support organizational change when used to reinforce behaviors that are in alignment with the organization's desired behaviors or outcomes.

As I said, a well-designed rewards system can reward the employee's job, the skill or the performance, or a combination of these. What is important is that the reward system needs to be tied to the performance that is desired from the employee and be considered fair when viewed from within the organization.

22 MANAGEMENT VS. LEADERSHIP SKILLS

At the management level you will be focusing on skills which will allow the organization to manage and control its internal the processes. These activities are important to the organization because they allow the organization to be efficient in its operations and effectively control the production, timing and cost of its various activities. There are certainly opportunities at this level to exhibit and exercise leadership skills, these competencies should be integrated with the management tasks which are important to the organization.

Management Skills

Managers are problem solvers who create goals to maintain to the stability of the organization. Individuals within the organization need to understand their roles, how their contribution leads to the overall success of the organization and the boundaries within which they can operate. Thus a manager's responsibility should focus on planning the various activities within her domain of control and organizing those people within their control to perform the work required within the organization's guidelines. The manager will make sure that the controls are in place to ensure the proper quality of the intermediate and finished product and communicate the progress of these activities in a meaningful way to the organization's higher-level management and, as appropriate, among the group members.

A successful manager will develop the appropriate tacit knowledge to efficiently engage and supervise his/her employees. These abilities are not always clearly explicit but include practical everyday experience. This professional intuition or 'practical knowledge' has been learned in previous positions and experiences, and enables the manager to adapt to changing and varied activities and experiences. This practical knowledge reflects the ability to learn from experience and apply that knowledge to other circumstances, creating adaptive responses to new problems and situations.

As previous chapters have identified many divisions within the modern organizations, managing within these various divisions is as varied as the tasks which need to be completed. Within these divisions the relative view of the manager is narrow in perspective, establishing processes and identifying routines, and monitoring the efficiency of daily or program operations. These processes tend to be formal and are implemented in a scientific and practical manner.

Leadership Skills

As I have indicated elsewhere, an individual can be a leader at any level by being a role model and motivating others to perform in alignment with the organization's goals. In order to be a leader at any level they need to have practical intelligence—

the ability to solve everyday problems utilizing experiential knowledge, purposefully adapting, changing environments and processes. Helping and motivating employees to achieve their individual activities efficiently falls under the concept of *transactional leadership*.

At a higher level a leader can help his employees improve their personal service delivery and adapt to changes and environmental shift (changes to the internal and external working environment). Helping employees understand and modify their behaviors to be successful in the new environmental conditions falls under the concept of *transformational leadership*.

Leaders inspire their peers and followers and help people see how their efforts can lead to improved personal and organizational growth. They move organizational development and facilitate change and improvement. Having studied the organization's environment and those things that drive the market, they hold a broad perspective about the organization and the role of the employees. They are constantly assessing the originations' and the individual needs and are looking for the best fit for both.

A good leader will be able to envision future and be constantly driving the organization toward adaptive change.

Leadership Skills

23 CRITICAL THINKING & DECISION MAKING

Congratulations! You are becoming successful and being given an opportunity to move into the upper management of the organization. To get here you have mastered the technical aspects of your industry, managed projects and groups of people to achieve program goals, and perhaps you have spent time in management positions within your organization, gaining experience with some of the business aspects of the organization.

As we begin to look at high-level skills, what I'm referring to as leadership skills, we will look at some of the processes that you may be involved in and how you can improve your skills and chances for success in your new position. I will introduce these processes to you so that you will begin to understand how your cognitive and emotional processes work and how they affect your ability to think clearly and make sound decisions.

In this chapter we will examine the related processes of critical thinking and decision making. In order to dig into these processes and their inherent sources of error, however, we must first look at the processes that we use to interpret information and infer conclusions about his information.

Data, Information, Interpretation

Let's start with raw data from the world. This data comes to us through our senses. As raw data (sounds, colors, etc.) we find associated patterns for this data, and begin to interpret the meaning of this data. Once we organize this data and associate it with meaning it becomes information. If we hear a gunshot we initially try to analyze this sound and direction (data). By comparing this sound with previous memories of sound we associate it with a gunshot (information). The next step for us would be to begin to determine whether it would be normal to hear a gunshot in this location, or whether someone may be interested in harming us (interpretation of the information).

Because we do not have the time (or resources) to go out into the world and collect accurate information about everything that we feel is important for ourselves we usually skip that step, and rely on people to go out in the world and collect information and sort it out for us. We usually seek information from those people who provide its own initial interpretation. Because we don't usually have the opportunity to seek two or more opposing sources of information we usually don't get balanced information interpretation. To follow the familiar food metaphor 'You are what you eat', your perspectives are comprised from the information you seek out and allow in.

Processing 'Rules'
When you were young someone showed you a picture of an apple and said the word and you began making an association of the word and the

picture. Eventually you were presented with one, and learned how to write the word 'apple'. All of these were associations and representations of the physical object which you assimilated as such.

In fact, everything that you know was taught to you in a similar way. Your teachers have been showing you pictures, examples, and written descriptions and you have made associates with these objects, ideas and perspectives. When you learned about more complicated perspectives, say slavery or communism, you likely have other emotional and value-judgment tags associated with them—good or bad, perhaps anger or frustration. These are based upon modern cultural interpretations (or re-interpretations) of these concepts.

During the Civil War period, individuals in the north and south (and indeed individuals on different sides of the color divisions) had very different perspectives on the rightness of slavery. These differences were so pronounced that there was a war fought to determine whether it should continue. (I realize that there was more to the Civil War, however I am using the concept to make a point.) This punctuates the famous saying that 'History books are written by the victors.'

These value associations are embedded through our cultural and learning processes. Students in a communistic country are taught a very different value association with the concept of communism than members of a capitalistic country. We get many of these tags and associations from our teachers, family members, friends and other associations, and the complex web of value associations among individuals varies as widely as people's learning experiences.

As you matured you were paying attention to the world, sorting information and learning basic 'rules' for how things worked and went together. When you were hurt and cried your mother would come and calm you. Things flying in the sky were birds. You have become very good sorting and associating things together and use these rules or *heuristics* to process information. As a matter of fact, you use these heuristics so efficiently that you commonly expect the things of the world to be organized in these patterns and are surprised to see that there are deviations from these rules. The first time I saw a PBS special on ducks I was surprised to see that there were diving ducks. Perhaps I had never seen one or learned that there were ducks that dived to the bottom of the lake, but I needed to modify my heuristic about ducks at that time to include the new data.

As you enter into your business you learn about the way things are normally organized and regulated, and learn the proper processes for accomplishing your tasks and for dealing with information, others within your organization and how the industry works (and perhaps should work). These heuristics allow you to work comfortably within your knowledge area, and become comfortable organizing and processing information. This is the cognitive version of a tacit skill—it is an automatic organizing process and happens on a subconscious level. These rules are so pervasive in your life that you are not aware of them—they have become a part of your learning and information processing structure and your personality.

Additionally, you have an additional source of built-in error. Let's say that you have a preferred news source. If you gather information from Fox News or Public Broadcasting you are going to get the information with the perspective from the source imbedded into it. Just the fact that some information is presented to you while other information is not presented biases the thoughts and interpretations that you will generate from the information. The fact that you seek information and interpretation from a particular source introduces a *bias* to the information. This bias will affect your perspectives of the world because of the information that you bring in and how it is interpreted. Data about the number of guns in the United States would have very different interpretations if presented by the National Rifle Association as opposed to presented by the Coalition to Prevent Gun Violence.

It is important to realize that very little information comes from the world without some type of interpretation, or bias. Because there is so much information available in the world we seek the information assimilated, interpreted and presented to us. The fact that we consistently go to the same sources gives us some comfort with the way the information is collected and presented. Again, almost all of the information that we receive has been interpreted for us at some level.

Sources of Error

Since the time of Plato people have been asking what 'truth' is. What is accurate information about our world? How can we begin to account for the inaccuracy of our data collection and interpretation? There are several sources of error that are naturally occurring in our observation and our thinking processes, our culture, self, and belief systems, and I'll begin to unpack these individually.

On the external level we are significantly influenced by our culture. Because our cultural norms are so imbedded in our information organizing and interpretation processes do not realize that we are using these heuristics. The modern metaphor is that of fish—if they could think and talk, how would you explain to them that they lived in the water? Because of their total immersion all of their life it would be difficult for them to understand a world outside of the world they knew. In the same way it is very difficult to study culture because it is so imbedded in our psyche we are unaware of the effects. It is considered that culture can only be studied by someone from outside the culture who could observe the differences (but only the aspects of the culture that would be different from their experiences).

According to Edgar Schein there are three levels of culture:
1. At the top are the *artifacts*, those aspects of the culture that you could observe and perhaps interpret. How do people behave toward each other? How do they respect their elders? Are they friendly toward each

other? Respectful? These are observable behaviors that can be interpreted together as general rules about the culture.
2. Below these artifacts are the *espoused values* that they hold. What are their collective goals and strategies for accomplishing these goals? What are their basic philosophies?
3. At the lowest level are the *basic underlying assumptions* that individuals of a culture collectively hold. What are their belief systems and how do these belief systems provide rules about how relationships should be organized. These beliefs are so embedded in the culture that they are taken for granted and not questioned. These are unconscious assumptions and are ultimately the sources of the group's values and actions.

We are therefore a source of error in our own interpretation of information. Because of our learning experience in the past, our friends, and our interpretation of our experiences we have our own ways of collecting and interpreting information. Our own personal biases for information sources and the fact that the information interpreted through our experiences and learnings, allow only certain perspectives into our consciousness.

Additionally, we interpret information based upon our own interpreted value system. When I see someone speaking harshly to someone else I interpret the actions based upon my own Christian perspective and value system. Because I have sensitivity for renewable energy and energy efficiency, when I walk into a place of business I interpret an incandescent lamp as being wasteful while others appreciate the warm color rendering of the lamp.

I have taken some time detailing the difference between data and information and our sources of error in interpretation of information so that we would have a foundation understanding how we collect and interpret information. This allows us to begin to look for strategies to seek to make our interpretation of information as un-biased as possible.

Critical Thinking

With all of the sources of error in our data collection and interpretation, how could we ever seek to understand whether our interpretations are accurate, or to understand other people's perspectives? Critical thinking skills are tools by which we can begin to improve our reasoning skills and determine the accuracy of our conclusions.

The concept of critical thinking represents a learned process whereby you begin to look at the information and processes that we use to receive, interpret and use data to reach conclusions. This process has several components, which are separated as follows:

1. What is the source of the data or information? Who collected the information? Is the information complete?
2. If the information came with interpretation, is it a reasonable interpretation? How can I identify the accurate information from the

source so that I can interpret the information and come to my own conclusion about the information?
3. What is the perspective of the author or group? Would the conclusions or interpretations that are presented represent the bias of the presenting group?
4. Is this information available from another source so that I can get the basic data and draw my own conclusions about the information?
5. Can I identify multiple sources of information and interpretation so that I can draw my own conclusions? This requires regularly seeking multiple information sources with (hopefully) contrasting perspectives.

As you can see, much of the critical thinking skills revolve around questioning the information source and trying to understand why the information was collected and interpreted as it was. Are there other ways to interpret this information? What are other possible perspectives?

This is the equivalent of walking around with a skeptical perspective all the time, questioning the sources and accuracy of the data and the perspectives of the people that are providing information and its interpretation for you. What is their perspective or interest in presenting the interpretation that they have? Have other people or groups interpreted the information and drawn the same conclusions? How can I independently verify the data and information and see if I draw the same conclusions? If you develop the regimen to continuously ask these questions you can develop the skills to question the interpretation (and sometimes the information) and begin to think critically.

Decision Making

Like the other aspects of our thought processes that affect our perspectives and evaluations, our decision making is also biased through standard decision-related patterns. Understanding these patterns can help you understand how to counterbalance these built-in processes to improve the quality and effectiveness of your decision-making.

Before we explore these standard processes, it is important to realize that our own personal differences will influence our decision-making beyond these patterns. If we are an optimistic person we may bias our decisions toward action whereas a pessimistic person may take a more conservative tact.

Additionally, the concept of *bounded rationality* expresses the idea that our access to and ability to process information is limited, and we will need to make a decision based upon this limited information. *Satisficers* will collect enough information to be comfortable that their decision is 'good enough' while *optimizers* will be seeking to collect enough information to optimize the decision.

The following is a partial list of standard decision-making and judgment biases and patterns:

1. Cognitive inertia—this is the same process that doesn't allow existing organizations to see new emerging technologies and trends as they could affect their ongoing business position. Individually, our 'view of reality' or expectations about how things are provide a filter for new information and do not allow us to conceptualize new alternatives and perspectives. People high in creativity are better at thinking 'outside the box'.
2. Confirmation bias or prejudice—we only see what we want to see. Information which conforms to our perspectives is embraced while information that does not fit our perspectives or desires is rejected. This perspective is the opposite of wishful thinking—where we seek and interpret information in accordance with our perspectives on how things should be.
3. Framing bias—a condition where your decision is related to how you perceive the opportunity. If you see it as a loss situation you may take a defensive/conservative position whereas if you see it as an opportunity for gain you will be more aggressive.
4. Search for information—our alternatives are often pre-selected by where we search for information about the alternatives. If we search in areas where we will not provide good information about alternatives we will obviously not obtain good information about selecting those alternatives.

5. Early termination of search—related to the above, if we obtain information which is 'good enough' we may make the decision without completely evaluating all the available information.
6. Recency—we have a tendency to place a higher weight on more recent information over more distal information.
7. Repetition bias compels us to apply additional weighting to information which we hear more often or which comes to us from different sources.
8. Anchoring—often we will anchor our perspectives on the initial information we obtain and then adjust our perspectives based upon the additional information we obtain.
9. Attribution bias—we have a tendency to attribute our successes to our own internal capabilities and performance where we attribute our failures to external factors (beyond our control). If something goes well, we take the credit; if something goes wrong we seek to blame other factors besides ourselves.
10. Additionally, groupthink is a group-related process whereby, through a process similar to peer pressure, you are inclined to conform to the general perspective of the group that you belong to.

Multiple Intelligences
As we leave the processes that affect our

perspectives and decision-making processes, we should at least consider the effect of our personal intelligence. Because g is a general intelligence measurement it does not fully evaluate the contribution of multiple dimensions of intelligence which affects our cognitive and emotional information processing.

Intelligence only represents the ability to perform analytical judgment. Individuals with high intelligence have the capacity to analyze multiple information channels and assimilate the information in accordance with previous patterns. They need to make a serious effort to be a critical thinker because of these embedded patterns, their heuristics. To compensate they need to pay particular attention to weighing details and not to make decisions quickly or based upon 'comfortable' information—consider and weigh all viable options.

Expertise can bias a response that is pre-programmed based upon the individual's experience. Experts and successful organizations can get stuck in conventional ways of thinking because of their previous success and miss new trends in the industry or new opportunities.

Creative people are good to have as a part of your decision-making group. They tend to defy the crowd, persevere in the face of obstacles, and take sensible risks. They have a tendency to see new creative alternatives and can conceptualize industry trends as they could be, not as they are.

Finally, wisdom is the ability to assimilate the information in practical ways. Wise people focus on solutions which will support the common good, and they do this by extending their field of vision beyond themselves to others, the organization, and the community. They are aware of and balance interests of various stakeholders.

    I hope that this section on our thinking processes and tendencies have been helpful in understanding our standard processes and heuristics. As we are able to understand how we tend to think we can put systems in place which will allow us to balance these biases and learn to make better quality observations and decisions.

24 SHIFTING SKILLS

One of the reasons that I wrote this book is so that young potential leaders could begin to look ahead and begin to understand and develop the competencies and skills that will allow them to be successful in future roles. Unfortunately, as you may have picked up from the preceding chapter, we are people that learn through the use of patterns. When we behave in a certain way and get a positive response or outcome we learn that that successful behavior is one that should be repeated. We rely on these comparisons to create rules for our behavior going forward.

As we progress through our technical, project management, managerial and potentially into our leadership roles, we have acquired skills and perspectives that have allowed us to be successful in these roles. In this chapter I will hopefully identify some of those rules which have allowed you to be successful in the past and should be re-evaluated or adapted in your new roles.

Career Growth

In your technical phase of your career you focused on developing and honing your technical skills, perhaps getting a professional license or certification, and providing proof that you had the minimum technical competencies to be recognized as a professional in your industry. Your life may have revolved around the technical solution to problems or performing high-quality services for your clients. You may have developed, sold or maintained equipment, components or otherwise provided detailed services for others. These were the years that you spent 'in the trenches'. I have always said that in order to manage others effectively (and certainly to lead them) you have to know what they are going through—you have to have had the experience in the trenches.

When you moved into early management you may have shared your time and responsibilities between your technical roles and project management roles, or you may have made the jump into project management and severed your technical responsibilities. In your new role you needed enough technical capability to be able to 1) understand what was being performed, and generally whether it was being done correctly, 2) organize individuals with technical experience to get the project complete within the project constraints, and 3) communicate the needs, process and progress to the project team, other outside stakeholders and the client. These are vastly different roles and require a shift (leap) from a technical focus to a holistic and integrated viewpoint. As a matter of fact, individuals that cannot disconnect from the technical design details cannot effectively manage—they never get their head out of the trenches and develop the capability to look holistically at a project and balance the multiple constraints of the project.

It is difficult to leave the technical and

detailed portion of the project delivery behind, especially for technically-oriented people. It is vital, however, in the shift to project management to be leaving those processes behind and developing and helping others to complete them. Project managers need to spend approximately 90% of their time communicating. They are responsible for making sure that all of the technical performance is happening in a coordinated way, managing the planning or execution of the project, monitoring the progress, integrating the reports from other groups, balancing scope change, budget accrual and schedule variation, communicating with the client and other key stakeholders, and continually passing important information among the team. The project manager is keeping a lot of balls in the air, and making sure that none of them are dropped. He/she is interested in the 'flow' of the project.

    The shift to a business management position could have happened gradually or suddenly as well, requiring a different set of skills. Managers are again often more narrowly and detail focused, and are looking at the processes being executed. Certainly there is a lot of communication going on, but the communication channels may be limited.

    The business manager is responsible for the effective performance of the individuals within their discipline group. He should be looking at the processes and identifying how they can be improved, how to measure the progress and how to improve the throughput or processes, and following important business metrics. He will be responsible for product his group's quality and accuracy as well as quantity, and may be responsible for identifying process improvements which will contribute to continuous process improvement.

In this role the business manager should be acutely aware of (or developing) the important process metrics which tells them that the process operations are happening in a predictable and appropriate manner. Depending upon the size of the group (and the organization) the exact role of the manager could vary greatly. Her communication is likely less in total volume but requires more professionalism. She may be responsible for communicating to upper management and still maintaining good communication horizontally and with subordinates.

Managers may be in the first position in their career where a part of their responsibility is to be aware of and responding to industry trends outside of the organization. As new processes and new technologies are introduced which may affect the way that their group performs or delivers their services, they need to understand these trends and be encouraging the organization to innovate and take advantage of these new opportunities.

Organizational Leadership

The transition into organizational leadership, which I consider the upper management of the organization, is soft transition, and may never happen at all. Because leadership can and should be present and exercised at all levels within the organization, these skills can be exercised at any time and any place within the organization.

Certainly by the time the manger reaches the top levels of management within the organization these leadership competencies and understandings should be present, and the organization's top management will be watching for them. There will still be managerial responsibilities and details to monitor, but the upper-level manager will begin having a larger view and perspective, have communication with the client asking them about the products and services that they desire, and how to be more effective at servicing their needs.

The organization exists in a changing environment, and the leader has a twofold responsibility; 1) to identify and understand the changes happening in the environment and with the perspectives of the customer and 2) to help the organization adapt to these changes. These adaptations may be technical (process and equipment) or cultural (learning new ways to do things). Change is often difficult for many people within the organization unless they can visualize a future state where they are successfully implementing new techniques and processes and seeing how it benefits them. This is how a leader can effectively lead the organization through change—allowing them to see how they can be effective by doing things differently.

Therefore, as you transition through your career path and are becoming aware of the skills and competencies which are important at the new level, be aware that the things that got you here won't get you to the next level. You will need to shift into strategic think processes. The detailed technical skills and behaviors that allowed you to be successful early must be displaced by new capabilities for viewing the organization and its programs holistically, metaphorically and in the context of the organization's environment and the client's needs. Once the need for change is identified your responsibility will be to help the organization map a strategy for adaptation. Finally, you will be helping employees understand how the organization can interface with them, exhibit empathy and support, and lead and support the organization and its members through environmental and adaptive organizational change.

25 SOCIAL INTELLIGENCE

In Chapter 17 we talked about developing personal Emotional Intelligence competencies. Considered a component of overall intelligence, we learned that our brains process emotional content at the same time and using the same processes as our cognitive processing. Our brains, hardwired millennia ago through evolution, relied on the emotional processing to queue the appropriate physical responses. As our world has changed we still process the emotional content in similar ways.

Previously we also looked at the personal competency concepts of self-awareness (how we process our feelings and emotions and how they affect our responses) and self-management (how we learn to control our drives and attitudes and insight into how we respond to emotional stimuli). These personal competencies allow us to engage with our world, our work, and others in a mature manner, maintain a positive attitude and focus, and respond appropriately to problems.

In this Chapter we will continue to build on Daniel Goleman's work as we explore the competencies around *Social Intelligence*—how to manage the social relationships with others in order to be successful. Like the personal competencies, these social competencies also can be organized into two groups—awareness and management. In the following sections we will look to at these competencies and gain insight into how we can learn to be more mature and effective in these social interactions.

This section focuses on your awareness of the social processes at work around you—at work, in the other relationships that you have, and in your wider world. Other people's perspectives and impressions of you are based upon not who you really are but rather by other people's impressions and observations of you, and the information that is available to them to evaluate you. What they see (including your actions) is what you are to them. Just as we constantly do to others, they are interpreting your behavior and communication (including, significantly, your non-verbal cues) and inferring your values, belief systems and qualities (honesty, integrity, friendliness, etc.) from these interactions.

Traits and Behaviors

As I have just indicated, people's perspectives of reality *are* their reality. Their perspectives of you are who you are to them. Presuming that you are not fraudulently presenting yourself as something that you are not, you need to cultivate traits about yourself that people can rely upon, be comfortable with, and not be threatened by.

An important attribute is *confidence* and its related characteristic, *composure*. By this point in your career hopefully you have had the opportunity to be in many comfortable (and perhaps some uncomfortable) work and social experiences, and have developed a successful perspective about these situations and learned from them. This should give you confidence that, whether or not the situation is similar to other situations you have been in, that you can successfully deal with new opportunities and threats that may present themselves. Other employees that have not had that experience look to you and your response for cues as to how to behave and whether to feel threatened.

Confidence allows you to walk into new situations and see similar patterns of behavior and opportunities to move forward. Because of your previous experiences you will have composure about yourself and be able to control your feelings and responses. Many of these high-tensions situations require similar behaviors; for many just taking time, pulling back, and considering rational responses. Your high-pressure situations in the past allow you to learn from the experience and envision responses that you would prefer in the future.

Because people will be looking up to you, you will need to be *self-motivated*, which will begin to drive the attitudes of others in the group. As people see you drive for self-improvement, to develop better processes at work, improve efficiency and communication, and enhance collaboration, they will be motivated to engage and participate themselves. People are looking to the leader to set the pace and compel them toward excellence. How do you engage the hearts of the others within the organization? Give them a model to inspire themselves and help them be a part of the team. As they achieve success in their activity/program level they will be motivated to participate at even higher levels, allowing you to advance yourself. This positive mental attitude is often developed and enhanced through the use of artful humor to pull down the defenses and make people feel more comfortable.

Because groups perform better (under most complicated circumstances) than individuals, building a *collaborative* attitude allows others to more comfortably participate in the development and decision-making process. Because they have been a part of the process of conceptualizing and developing the program and path forward, team members will be more highly motivated to engage and participate in the process.

When working with teams and groups of people, be aware of their emotional states. If you can, keep thoughts and conversations in a positive light and avoid negative emotions and tones. Good moods drive motivation toward increased productivity, quality and engagement in the improvement process. When people are engaged the quality of their decision making is improved through creativity and optimism, and when teams are involved the ability to leverage this goodwill is enhanced. When these positive mental attitudes are pervasive in the organization and translate into superior customer relationships you have achieved a significant goal.

Finally, your peers are looking to see *wisdom* in your behaviors and intuition. Wisdom is that combination of intellectual processing (knowledge) and the practical applications of this knowledge (common sense). If you have a position of power, people want to know that your decisions are in the best interest of the group, and if you don't have good practical common sense there can be a lot of concern about the direction that you are taking your group and company.

Social Awareness

If you can become aware of the social impressions that you make with others you can begin to influence the impressions that others have about you, potentially improving your relationships and maximizing the outcomes of these relationships. The management of your social interactions begins with an awareness and understanding of your feelings and attitudes that you may be projecting.

First, your personal feelings of *empathy* has two components—your ability to sense the emotions in others and to understand the emotions that the others may be feeling. This is an important aspect of your deep relationship with others—they need to feel the emotional connection with you. Much of our work lives happens at a blinding rate as people are becoming busier at work and continuing to work longer hours. An increasing amount of time is spent in and among our co-workers, and our ability to empathize with them and connect with them provides a foundation for deep relationships in the future.

Additionally, sensing other's emotions helps us understand who they are and how they will feel about our behaviors and actions, and how we can work with them effectively. Taking an active interest in their lives validates them and their feelings, and provides a good foundation for a deep relationship with them.

These personal relationships will allow you the opportunity to identify and address their needs and concerns. As you begin to be in a position of influence and leadership, people want to know that you care. If you understand their feelings and concerns but don't do anything to support them you are not benefitting them and they will not feel that you care. The empathy opens the opportunity to get in there and find ways to support those people at work that you care about.

Your awareness of the feelings and attitudes of your co-workers is important, but on a larger side you also need to have an awareness of the organization's culture and values. What do the members of the organization hold important, what are their goals (espoused and informal) and how are they striving collectively toward these goals. What is the formal decision process and how are the decisions really made and executed? What are the nuances of the organization's culture and value system, and how do people share power within the organization.

Your ability to understand the organization's power structure, decision processes and work and cultural processes allows you to help other people realize their goals in the organization. You also will have the opportunity to exert social influence when you understand and develop relationships with the important people with informal power and the gatekeepers within the organization.

Relationship Management

Having the ability to understand the organization's goals, how decisions and actions are implemented within the organization, and having developed relationships with the people at key points within the organization, you have the opportunity to influence the processes and outcomes of the organization. Because people under different circumstances respond to different stimuli, your ability to influence others will be impacted by your relationships and understanding of the organization's processes. You can influence decisions and perspectives among people within the organization if you can understand the organization's dynamics and the individual personalities involved and utilize the appropriate influence tactics.

Through these processes you can begin to institute and support change within the organization and help the organization adapt during important periods of environmental change. This visioning and influence process will recur in our conversation under leadership processes, but they are imbedded in the understanding of the organization's culture, values, processes and the feelings and attitudes of those organizational members who will be critical to embracing change.

Through your understanding of the individuals and their strengths you have the opportunity to help others develop and grow. As we will discuss in Chapter 26, it is difficult to provide corrective (negative) feedback, however if you have established the proper relationships with the individuals and you approach the feedback tactfully you can help people grow through positive and corrective feedback.

Additionally, all effective organizations work through processes of teamwork and collaboration. Helping to facilitate and support effective teams as a team member provides the goodwill and relationships that will allow people to look up to you when it is your turn to provide group leadership. By incorporating the values of cooperation and teamwork in your organizational life you establish your personal values and send a signal to others that you will expect them to behave in a similar manner at appropriate times.

Finally, if you have developed the proper relationships within the organization, have understood the process of influence and decision processes within the organization you can begin to provide leadership to the organizational members. People will adapt to organizational change if they can envision the benefits of the future state and they trust the leader. If you can establish yourself as a having goodwill, insight and the best interest of all the organizational members you can begin to exert influence toward the key organization's goals.

26 ROLE OF EXECUTIVE COACH

I have said that, through the various stages of your career development and growth, you will need to develop and utilize new and different skill sets. Initially, a mentor will help you 'learn the ropes', or provide useful information about the processes that your organization utilizes, the 'way things work'. As we will describe later in this section, the higher you go on the career ladder the more un-scripted these rules are, and the more you will need to utilize personal and leadership skills, which are not so easily learned. At the higher levels, the acquisition and effective use of these more complex personal skills can be enhanced through the use of an executive coach.

The root of the word *coach* derives from a 'vehicle to take someone somewhere'. As in sports, the coach's goal is to identify skills and strategies which will make you successful in your future position and then help you acquire those skills. Presuming that the coach has a larger view of the skills and behaviors that you would need at a particular (presuming high level) career stage, coaches are most effective when both the coach and you are highly motivated to grow. For this reason, it is important for the coach to see the big picture, know where you are, and where you are going, and what you need to be successful in the new position.

Coaching can work on multiple levels, so it

can truly have a wider context than individual coaching. Effective coaching can happen on a group level—trying to understand the dynamics within a group and how to adopt more effective processes. It can also happen at an organizational level—when the organization's leadership is dysfunctional, needs improvement, or is out of sync with the rest of the organization. Also, during times of significant environmental change, it is important to have the organization identifying these changes and positioning the organization for the new environmental conditions. All of these processes can fall under the concept of coaching, or perhaps organizational consulting at a company-wide level.

Although it is not often described as such, one fundamental aspect of coaching is to discuss and understand the work-life balance. Future goals, responsibilities and roles for a new leader need to match their personal preferences and their own personal goals. If this is not considered up front you could build a leader that cannot be effective because their personal goals, home life and personality do not align with the new role they are being introduced to.

Stress is also a significant factor that plays into every life at some level, sometimes wrecking an individual's health by triggering diseases and unhealthy behavior patterns, and sometimes bridging the work-life boundaries. The coaching relationship should introduce and help the future leader understand their new role, the physiological and psychological aspects of stress, and how the two can be effectively managed.

The higher you go the more the 'soft skills' are important. Because your technical roles were pretty well defined (either by the organization or by the profession) your success in these technical roles had fairly clear paths. As you got into project management and management these roles became more adaptive to the clients' preferences and needs, your team and your organization's capabilities and strengths, and the dynamics of the project delivery process. As you move into organizational leadership, your leadership and interpersonal relationship skillsets will, among others, leverage your ability to work with others, become an effective leader, remove obstacles and enable your subordinates, become a good listener and speaker, read the organization and its environment and bring about adaptive changes to the organization to be effective in the future. This final group of skills is not clearly defined, is subjective, and needs to be adaptive to the people you are working with and the environmental constraints at the time. This is where coaching, from a seasoned professional, can help. After all, how many successful athletic departments or teams do not have a coach?

The real value to this process is the discovery of new talents and abilities through the coaching process. If you can identify new skills that are valuable to the organization it is a win-win relationship for both the organization and the leader. Progressive and learning organizations are always looking for new talent and leadership skills!

These coaching relationships can span from a fairly pragmatic relationship to a psychotherapy process. Depending upon the relationship between the coach and leader, sometimes processes are open and sometimes they are closed (and private). Because the leader may be really digging into their personal preferences, belief systems and behaviors, the relationships between the coach and the leader are often kept confidential, and the communication with the organization's leadership may talk about progress toward the organization's communicated goals and soliciting feedback from the organization on progress.

The Process

The coaching process involves several different stages:

1. Everything begins with the coach's understanding the organization's culture and expectations and the new role for the person being coached. In your role as an a leader your new position will require an intersection of your skills (current and future) and the organization's culture, which provides the environment or the context that those skills will be working within. Your success in being coached for a new position requires an accurate assessment of the skills you need and how those skills fit with the organization's needs and what will be effective. This is the 'where you are going' portion of the metaphor. If the destination is not accurately identified, you may be taken somewhere you don't want to go. Often these proposed skill targets are reviewed

and/or approved by other organizational leaders to be sure that the coaching process is heading in a good direction that we have an accurate goal established.

It is important to note that coaches come with their own worldview, perspectives, heuristics and strategies that have worked for them in the past. In order to effectively assist you in being effective in your new role, either the lessons from these past experiences will be effective for your learning experience or they need to get out of their 'box' and develop new adaptive strategies for your new circumstances and position. To play with our metaphor once more, coaches have (presumably) been to the destination before, and as long as the destination is good for you as well, they can use the same strategies or 'maps'. If your destination is unique, they need creativity and intuition in order to develop and utilize a new and un-scripted map.

2. The next stage is the *assessment* of your current skills mapped against the skills identified in the previous section. Where are your current skill sets? Because the coaching process involves taking someone from where they currently are to where they want to go (at least the coach's or the leader's perspective on where that is), an effective strategy for 'how to get there' begins with 'where we are'.

This assessment often comes through interviews with your peers, supervisors, and managed employees. From these interviews the effective coach can identify skills, habits and preferences that you have developed and identify weaknesses that may hold you back.
3. Comparing the required skills with the skills that you have, the coach will go through a process often identified as a *gap analysis*, or identifying the skills that you need that you currently don't have or that need to be developed. At a lower level in your career, this wasn't difficult because many of the skills were technical and pretty clearly defined. Project management and general management were also somewhat clearly defined; however your effectiveness in these areas began to leverage more on your soft skills, your interpersonal effectiveness. As you work into a leadership role within the organization these soft skills will be your key to success and failure within your new role.
4. From this gap analysis the coach will develop an action plan—a list of activities and goals to be striving for. These often begin with an awareness of behaviors and attitudes that are detrimental and that should be extinguished. Next goals of self-improvement and personal or group effectiveness would be developed.
5. Now is the hard part—*implementation*. Your attitude as an emerging leader, how well you

embrace the learning process and your motivation will determine your success. Starting with the extinguishing of behaviors that are not effective, once success or improvement has been established in these areas it is possible to begin looking at growing some of the high-level leadership skills.

6. Feedback and continually adapting the learning process will lead to the ultimate success of the coaching relationship. As a leader you need to be accountable for the acquisition and development of behaviors which will be effective and always on the alert of negative feelings and perspectives which could limit your effectiveness.
7. Because the environment is always changing, the organization seeks new goals and adapts, and our peers have growing expectations, a periodic follow-up with a coach often helps identify adaptations that will allow you to become increasingly more efficient.

A leader's development should happen at his/her own comfortable pace. The leader needs to be able to experiment with strategies and determine what works for them, adapt their behavior toward others as it is comfortable for them, and solicit feedback from others as to how their new behaviors work and are being received. This provides less stress to the adaptive process and is more comfortable for the leader. If the initial processes are to remove dysfunctional behavior and the individual is able to effectively make progress in these areas this initial success may instill self-confidence and motivate the adoption of some of the more subjective and difficult skills and behaviors. It also takes time for the others within the organization to become comfortable with adapted behaviors.

Feedback Quality

You have heard the term 'garbage in, garbage out'. Soliciting and receiving accurate feedback is the key to improvement. If you don't get good feedback or you don't have good strategies for improvement, you won't be able to make effective progress. Any coaching or mentoring process will be ineffective or could be detrimental without accurate feedback.

People vary in their capacity to receive and process criticism. Because of our ego and self-perspective biases, we have an inflated view of ourselves and attribute much of our success to ourselves and our capabilities. What has been helpful for me to understand is that the skills that brought you success through your previous professional phases are not the skills which you need going forward. Keeping in mind that you are developing new skills for the new roles will help you become more open to and to embrace the feedback and coaching processes.

Strategic Focus

The key to an organization's effective business strategy is that their leadership team needs to have an accurate understanding of the organization's environment, a good understanding of their collective skills and competencies, and take the appropriate action in order to be successful. Misreading the environment can have a significant effect on the organization's viability and profitability, and may cause the organization to miss important cues opportunities. One of the goals of a good coach will be to reinforce behaviors which can lead to environmental scanning, identifying trends and being proactive about communicating these observations.

Because we human beings come with heuristics and biases, and many of these are so engrained in our psyche that we do not realize that we have them, it affects our assessment of the organization and the environment. Because we attribute so much of our successes to ourselves and our organization we may miss the major trends and opportunities in the environment as well as within our organization. One of the roles of the coach is to identify these 'blind spots' and recommend processes and feedback to ensure that they are mitigated.

In this light, a good coach can help introduce the concept of contingency planning. Through the project management process you likely learned the value of risk identification and risk management. Businesses are subject to the same type of risk from the wider economy. If you have been around a while you have witnessed a recession or two. They come without warning and significantly shift the industrial and commercial output of the economy. New terms are being introduced into our vocabulary fairly regularly— super storm, derecho, polar vortex, etc. How well positioned is your organization to ride through economic and other 'disasters' which may affect your region. In particular, organizational management tends to miss or not effectively respond to long-term declines or shifts in the industry because they do not deviate significantly from the 'norm' that they are used to in order to trigger a response.

Organizational Change
A special case for coaching/consulting is organizational change. If the environment shifts and the organization needs some assistance 1) identifying the changes, 2) helping the organizational develop an adaptation strategy and 3) helping the organization implement the needed changes, an outside coach can often help. Because they are not immersed in the culture and the rigid perspectives of the organizational environment on a daily basis they can provide an independent lens for looking at the problem asking appropriate questions and holding people accountable for the change goals that were identified.

Learning Organization
Organizational learning is the democratization of growth and development within an organization. To be effective, organizational learning processes can begin anywhere in the organization where someone identifies a problem,

process improvement or opportunity within the environment. Organizations must be programmed to listen to this input, process it, and identify the issue as a significant trend, opportunity for process improvement or random information. Learning organizations are able to identify trends in the industry, prepare appropriate responses and implement corrections faster than their competition, which gives them the competitive advantage.

If an organization does not have processes in place to enable communications and the processing of valuable information at all organizational levels, the coach can help the organization create processes to engage its employees and follow through on opportunities that are identified.

At this point we have talked about many of the processes behind the leadership transition. Going forward we will take on these leadership behaviors and attitudes which will allow you to be successful in this new role.

27 LEADERSHIP PROCESSES

This is a book on leadership. Why am I not getting to leadership till Chapter 27? Because leadership is a complex subject and has a lot of moving parts. As we have been talking about helping others, team focus, emotional intelligence and other similar topics we have been talking about leadership from a foundational standpoint. So what is 'leadership'? As my philosophy professor used to say to me, 'let me begin to unpack it for you'…

If you have been to a bookstore, taken a class in leadership or had an in-depth dialog about leadership you will know that it does not have a simple definition or an agreed-upon set of behaviors or character traits. There are behavior sets which have been defined and developed over time, been modified, and expanded in order to refine the concept of leadership, but there are as many perspectives on leadership as there are theories to be researched. To further complicate the definition there are lots of quotes concerning leadership such as "Leadership is hard to define but you know it when you see it."

For the sake of the journey we are taking together, I will choose to define leadership as the interaction between the leader, the followers and the situation that allows the followers to be motivated toward the leader's goals. This definition allows us to explore several different aspects of our concept of leadership.

Multiple Theories

If you open a college textbook on leadership they will begin to identify traits and behaviors which are important to the study of leadership. We will probably identify many of these behaviors, but I will try to set them into a professional context and provide the direct application for these behaviors.

Any of these theories that focus on the individual only can explain only a part of the story, and don't take into consideration the perspectives and feelings of those that are following the leader and the situation that they are in. The relationship between the leader and the followers are defined by these interrelationships, and I believe that the effective leader can develop an awareness of the situations and develop and implement effective leadership behaviors and responses that are appropriate to these various situations. In the following section we will dig into these relationships under the heading of situational leadership.

Contingency Theory or Situational Leadership

From a practical standpoint, this theory allows for multiple relationships between leaders and followers based upon the situation and the interplay between them. The first and most important component of the process is the contribution of the leader. In any particular situation there are aspects of the leader which motivate the followers to put forth their energy and talents toward achieving the leader's goals. These goals may or may not be articulated, but the goals or at least the path forward must be clear to the followers. Most leadership studies and theories concentrate on the leader's skills and abilities to motivate the followers toward the goal, and recognize that the followers must have comfort with the leader's personal abilities and personality to apply their energies toward the goal.

The second aspect of leadership that we will explore is the perspective of the followers, who are putting their effort forth to achieve the leader's goal. It could be assumed that, on average and over time, the level of effort that is put forth toward the goal is based upon their perception of the leader and the worthiness of the goal. This will be controlled by their motivation, which will be based upon their perception of their individual reward for their contribution toward the goal, their own personal drive, and perhaps due to their perspectives toward the team. There are also dynamics of power in any relationship, which can be embodied by, among others, position power or charismatic power. The effective leader-follower relationship is also built upon trust and respect. Finally, the follower's level of effort expended and duration of this effort contribution may be driven by other aspects of the follower's perception of the leader.

The third aspect of this leadership relationship is the situation, what is referred to as the "environment"—the world that the relationship is built within. There are two significant aspects of this environment which should be discussed at this point—the organization (micro) and the organization's environment (macro). Whether an individual is working as a sole proprietor or within a small or large organization, this organization has a culture—a set of rules of behavior that is expected or "normal" for the situation. These behaviors are embedded within the organization and are learned when a new employee joins the organization. Presuming that the individual is happy within the organization she/he has accepted or agreed to behave in accordance with some or most of the cultural "norms" of the organization.

Additionally, the organization operates in an environment. In any business, their competitive advantage waxes and wanes over time, and government, political, seasonal and technological changes affect the organization's ability to operate efficiently and profitably over time. This environment can affect the organization positively, causing the organization stress to produce products in a volume and a timely manner as required, and can also starve the organization of resources required to maintain itself in the manner to which it is organized.

Thus, in this example, we have our concept of leadership built upon the premise that a leader motivates a group of followers to achieve a goal in a particular context (comprising the intra-organization's environment and the organization's external environment). As we look to develop the concept of leadership within this chapter we will explore each of these areas in more detail.

The Leader

The leader is the aspect of this triad which is most often studied and explored, and has the most history behind its theories. There are leadership theories which focus on the attributes, behaviors and motives of the leaders. In this book I have identified several aspects of leadership that I believe are important to be included in a discussion of leadership in a professional context. Many of these you will (hopefully) recognize from behaviors which I have been trying to focus on as you develop through your professional career stages.

1. *Respect and integrity.* Any leader which rises from within the organization brings their collective personal experiences with other employees, clients and others outside the organization. All of these speak to the integrity of the future leader. If other employee's experiences with the leader through the developing period in his/her career were negative it will be difficult to change these perspectives and win the respect of those within the group that have been mistreated in the past. From this perspective, you will reap what you sow.

   As a professional your reputation will be your most important attribute both within the organization and without. Many companies have the opportunity to make their purchasing decisions based upon their perception of the leader's perceived capability and integrity. Because professional relationships are established based upon a relationship of trust, the perspective of personal integrity provides the foundation for the development of other business relationships.

2. *Communication skills*. From the time that you were involved in Project Management you have spent most of your time communicating with others, whether or not you wanted to. Often your role was that of the interpreter—identifying the perceived needs of the clients, explaining to them the processes and information about their needs, and interpreting the tasks required to others within your organization to perform the work and achieve the desired outcomes. You have also been the liaison with other key stakeholders in the process.

I used to be frustrated by the fact that I spent so much of my time communicating with and managing the perceptions of the other employees until I finally determined that, as a leader within the organization that was my job. As I began to relax into my management and leadership responsibilities I became more comfortable working with others to achieve project and organizational goals and having them become comfortable with the process.

Deep communication involves active listening and really tuning into the other person(s) in the dialog. Much of my early communication was transactional—just getting communication done so we can get back to our important job at hand. It wasn't until I started really connecting with others, seeing where the come from and what their goals and perspective were, that I got beyond the transactional and could develop solutions and agreements that provided not only the response I wanted but the beneficial feelings and attitudes of the employees.

3. *Critical Thinking Skills*. Along with social intelligence, critical thinking skills are a primary competency of an excellent leader. I love the adage that 'The person that knows how to do something will always have a job, and they will be working for the person that knows why.' As you were learning your technical skills and to provide project management and delivery you were learning the 'how' processes—how to achieve valuable outcomes and avoid pitfalls for the client, which provided valuable returns for the organization. Your value to the organization was based upon the value of the project(s) that you delivered, the relative value of these projects to the client, and the scarcity of these services in the local environment. You were able to receive personal returns based upon the value of the project and the complexity and the personal intensity required for the delivery.

As you moved up in the organization you were provided more oversight and responsibility, which required accommodating to existing processes and (hopefully) developing new processes which provided increased efficiency and the use of newly developed tools. This space was likely still very structured and organized.

When you moved into upper organizational leadership, your responsibilities were much less structured. Developing organizational strategy means understanding the organization and its environment, reading technologies and future trends and understanding how they affect the organization, and developing strategies for moving the organization into the future. Beyond that, your organization has momentum—it knows how to do what it has done very well and people have become comfortable with these processes and working relationships. Adaptation to new technologies or a shifting environment require organizational change—something that does not come easy.

Critical thinking skills are the ability to think outside of the box—the way things have been done in the past. The 'box' is your set of personal heuristics, biases and worldviews, and is significantly related to those of your friends and peers. These boxes affect the way that we look at the world, process data and make decisions.

On the day before Apple came out with the iPhone, virtually every telephone had buttons on it. It takes creativity and the ability to analyze new technology platforms that are emerging, and imagine a creative use to adapt new technologies or to solve an existing (or potential) problem or opportunity.

Critical thinking is often expressed by the concept of *perspective*. This can include getting outside of not only your organization but your world. It is very interesting to see how people in other cultures value work/home relationships, conduct business, use energy use, respect family, express theology and social norms and incorporated them into very functional social relationships. This wider perspective allows for the evaluation of information through a different lens. If you could always view a new situation from the perspective of 'why not' or 'that's interesting' you would have the opportunity to expand your realm of what is possible.

Critical thinking requires an ongoing awareness and sense of mindfulness. It begins with a process of being aware of your thoughts and perspectives and how they provide interpretation to the information you are receiving. You can begin to monitor and understand how your mind works—where your perspectives and biases come from, and decide whether to accept those mental interpretations or not. If not, just identifying other conceptual options and perspectives, and validating those other perspectives, helps move you out of the mental frames that you hold. Frames are very difficult to remove completely, because they are constructed from your value systems and culture, however by questioning the perspective you hold and the reasoning you use you can begin to at least understand your biases and the way that you arrive to conclusions.

Organizations want their strategic leader to hold the perspectives and understanding of the industry, but be able to see new emerging trends and opportunities. Leaders with developed critical thinking skills can at least understand their own thought- and decision-processes and use this knowledge to maintain mindfulness about the potentially creative and 'non-traditional' interpretation of information.

4. *Emotional Control.* We have talked extensively in earlier chapters about the developed ability to monitor and control your emotions. This is much easier said than done, and I've struggled with this all my life. The bottom line is people want their leaders to be acting rationally, making good decisions, and not getting frustrated or

overcome with stimuli. Emotional maturity requires people to be aware of and monitor their emotional status and how it affects their ability to think and respond appropriately.

People with a low ability to control their emotions tend to 'flood' or allow their emotions to drive their processing ability. This can be demonstrated in rage, shut-down or inappropriate responses, but leaders are expected to remain composed, calm and able to make appropriate judgments about important decisions and difficult situations.

5. *Social Sensitivity*. This includes the ability to understand where the social counterpart (client, employee, or peer) is emotionally and exhibiting the correct behavior in order to get the appropriate response from them. People in the sales side of the business tend to be good at identifying where people are and when they may be ready for the pitch. A good leader will understand where his counterpart is, and work the conversation (including emotional content) toward the goals that they have for the outcome. This begins with learning you're your counterpart is, understanding what the foundation of their beliefs or desires are, and working your perspectives into the flow of the conversation in a convincing way.

6. *Empathy*. People want to know that you care about them. Whether you are a

customer, employee or other stakeholder, you want to know that people have your best interests and perspective at heart. To accommodate this the leader needs to be approachable—you want to know that if there is a significant issue or concern that you are able to share it and at least have them acknowledge your concern and deeply consider the issue.

7. *Vision & Mission around People.* We get a lot of information from the organization's goals and mission. What do these statements say about the organization's important members, their needs and goals? How is your organization organized? How the rewards distributed and what are the opportunities for advancement? Do these processes seem fair on the inside?

The leader needs to drive these processes and programs to reflect their personal feelings about the employees and their growth and development. How the rewards are distributed says a lot about the equity, fairness and empathy that an organizational leader has for his/her followers.

Does the leader really have the organization's members at heart? Are there continuing education programs, appropriate benefits and other systems in place to identify and support employee growth and wellness?

8. *Give Away Power*. As we will discuss in the later sections, whether followers are motivated to follow a leader is driven significantly by the situation. There are situations that require the power to be concentrated at the top (as when there is a major threat to the organization or some significant or emergency response is required). Most of the time, however, new emerging leaders and young managers need to be 'empowered' to be able to attempt and learn new leadership roles and responsibilities.

   Leaders that concentrate power and exercise command-and-control structures aren't really leaders, they are managers. They have the power to command action and provide rewards, and thus they won't be effectively engaging and motivating anyone.

   Good leaders are open to allow others to grow and develop, creating a foundation for the organization to develop a wider base and new skill sets. In order for an organization to grow they either need to import top talent or grow it. Proactive organizations and leaders are always looking for talent and learning opportunities.

   The Followers
   As important as the feelings and behaviors of the leader are, the follower(s) must be receptive to and motivated by these same attributes.

Interestingly, these followers come from different organizations, cultures and life experiences, and thus they draw their own unique perceptions of what is important to them.

Thus the leader must understand the followers' collective and individual motivations and value systems, and must work with them at their individual level. If the goal is to motivate the employees toward the collective goal, the collective goal must be perceived to be in line with the individual's goals and values. This goal must be worthy of putting effort forth to achieve, and the value to them must be perceived to be at least worth their efforts to achieve the goal.

The concepts of Equity Theory tell us that the individuals need to feel comfortable that the returns that they are receiving for their time and efforts are appropriate among their peers and within the industry, balanced by the local cost of living and other conditions in their lives. Notice that I used the term "feel", for this relative valuation can be as subjective as it is objective—does the social contract between the organization and the individual seem to be 'fair'.

An important factor to a young, motivated professional's life is the opportunity for advancement. The motivated individual must be able to see an upward path for themselves in the organization in order to feel secure in their position into the future. If the organization does not provide (or the individual cannot conceptualize) this upward path or make it accessible then the individual may choose to leave and seek their success in a new organization or on their own.

Some followers leave the organization or the leader. As we will see in the next section, some individuals joining the organization have trouble adopting or accepting the organization's culture, goals, values, personalities or other aspects of the organization. Sometimes the individual or the organization miss-judges their capabilities and has a hard time selling the individual's skills and competencies in the organization's environment or to their clients. Recognizing that all individuals that join an organization do not stay for their full working careers, attrition is a significant aspect of the organization's life, and the organization's cultural perspectives associated with employees leaving is an important aspect of the organization's ability to be open, honest and comfortable with their employees.

Let's be honest—do most employees of an organization feel motivated to achieve a common, organizational goal or are they working in a social contract to exchange some hours of their time for the organization in exchange for a financial return established by the industry? This 'social exchange platform' is embedded in the capitalistic model and is supervised by the organization's management. This situation is very common at the task level, but highly talented individuals with potential will soon be looking for higher value returns and an appropriate outlet for their talents. If the organization cannot provide it, they will seek elsewhere for their satisfaction.

The Situation

Effective organizational leadership happens in a particular type of situation or *context*. There are two important dynamics associated with the situation which should be weighed: the organization itself and the environment in which the organization exists.

If you recall, an organization can be considered a group of individuals that have joined together in order to fill a need within their community or environment. Organizations take the knowledge, skills and abilities of the individuals working within the organization in order to provide a service to their customers. They add value to the individual by taking their capabilities and combining them with the capabilities of other employees to produce and deliver a product or service to the customer. The individual may have skills that may or may not have high individual value in the industry, but when combined with the skills of others they are able to achieve a higher return or value from their efforts.

I realize that many individuals do not think about the 'contract' that they have with their employer—the exchange of time and effort for an hourly wage or other means of compensation. These concepts are buried within the over-arching schema of capitalism as it is currently played out within the free world, and most individuals do not consider themselves as a part of the free exchange processes active in the world. There is at the root of every employment contract, however, the concept of equity which the organization (employer) needs to balance with the individual (employee) to make them satisfied with their work situation.

Not to get bogged down into the concept of the individual and the organization, it is important to note that an organization is, by law, a socially constructed "individual". Constructed from a group of individuals who may have resources or access to a market, this "individual", which we term an organization (either for-profit or non-profit and seeking other goals) this organization can acquire and own real property, including land, and can hire and discharge employees, and can earn and distribute profit, and be taxed. If we take the metaphor of the 'organization as an individual' to the next logical step, we know that different individuals have different motivations, means for achieving their goals, and perceptions about the world. In a sense, we are talking about the individual's *personality* and *value systems*.

In a similar manner to the individual's personality, organizations have personalities as well, but we refer to them as the organization's 'culture' or 'climate'. For the sake of this book we will refer to the organization's culture as their way of doing things, and are based upon the organization's value systems, often referred to as their "core values" and are often referred to in the organization's mission or vision statements. The organization's culture is a collective embodiment of the things that the organization feels are important and is portrayed in the day-to-day interactions of the individuals within the organization.

Individuals that are attracted to the

organization will, upon joining, confront these cultural attitudes as reflected in the behaviors of the organization's members. Presuming that these cultural attitudes are in alignment with the individual's own individual personality and value system they will be complimentary and the individual will feel comfortable within the organization. If the individual and the organization's behaviors are not compatible the individual may try to adapt or change their perspective or may petition for change within the organization. Either way there will be tension within the individual and the organization.

Because an organization's culture drives the accepted (and not acceptable) behaviors within and among the individuals, motivations and goals of the individuals, attitudes and perspectives about clients, peer organizations, the community and their social responsibility, they establish the important dominant perspectives of organizational life. These behaviors have a foundation in the core values of the organization (whether or not formally articulated) and as embodied and adapted by the individuals within the organization, through both formal and informal processes.

Final Thoughts

There are other aspects of leadership which have been brought forth in the current research and which should considered while building a holistic perspective of the leader, her value system or standard behavior patterns.

1. *Transparency*. Followers in an enlightened age are interested in knowing where you are taking them. What are your value systems, goals, vision and intentions? Organizational members watch the leader and are interested in the leader's behavior, inferring their intentions. In an open culture and especially with the newer generations, employees want to participate in and be a part of the organization. Certainly there are aspects of the organization which should not be widely shared, but the followers want to see the leader, watch the leader as she works toward their goals, report their progress, and talk about successes in addition to challenges. Taking the time to explain the good and bad developments empowers the others within the organization. Social media helps provide a vehicle to celebrate successes, but must be actively managed.
2. *Organizational culture* is an important aspect of the organization's attractiveness and appeal. Aspects of an organization's appear very quickly to new applicants or entrants—and can provide a solid appeal to applicants and current employees. Employees with high level talent can take their skills elsewhere if they don't see themselves staying with your organization. Part of your responsibility is to establish the value system and baseline treatments which will allow a positive culture to develop within the organization. If you have an

opportunity, slow down the processes of value selection and have the organization's members participate in developing the organization's culture (they will anyway). This sense of fundamental democracy can allow you to attract high value candidates and keep high value employees.

3. *Create a 'buzz'.* It is one thing to have employees and clients that are happy with your services and it is another to have them talking among their peer groups. One way to create the buzz around your work and activities is to use social media, and another is to be in a prominent position in other organizations within your community. If you are doing things outside the norm for your industry you can get people talking about you. Be known as the innovator and the one that gets things done, and clients and good employees will be attracted to your organization.

4. *Create a team environment.* We talked about this earlier in the book, but the same principles apply here. If you can identify ways to celebrate team (organizational) successes and provide rewards for the team and not just the individual you will not create a competitive environment but a synergistic one. People learn that their processes go well and they achieve valuable outcomes when they work well with others and they begin to enjoy their work and their peers.

5. *Creativity* is a difficult skill to teach but important to have as a part of your organization. Creative people are able to generating ideas and products that are novel, high quality and often very appropriate to the task. Because leaders, as they grow within their industry, they view the industry within the existing structures or lenses and apply solutions and strategies which have been successful in the past. Creative people will be able to look at problems and opportunities with new lenses, are able to generate ideas 'outside the box'. Through their creative processes they redefine problems, which allow them to be viewed more as opportunities than problems. Sometimes stepping away from a problem and not requiring a forced solution allows for a synthesis of ideas and a re-definition of the situation and potential options.
6. *Courage*—be willing to take sensible risks and do things which are novel and creative to be able to see what sort of response the market might have for these ideas. As long as it is not seen as foolish within the organization it goes a long way to encourage innovation.
7. Be on the lookout for and pay attention to those individuals with *wisdom*, that practical knowledge (remotely correlated with g, not necessarily correlated with leadership). Wisdom includes a collection of factors 1) rich factual knowledge, 2) procedural

knowledge, 3) practical knowledge about strategies of judgment & advice about the matters of life, 4) understanding about the context of life and temporal relationships, 4) relativism (differences between goals values & priorities) and 5) uncertainty. Wise people balance experience and intuition to conceptualize options which are beneficial for the organization.

8. Watch out for signs of an *inflated ego*, which can have a negative effect on your attractiveness as a leader, it undermines your decision quality and is a barrier to deep relationships. An inflated personal perspective leads to inflated optimism about your outcomes and decisions, egocentrism, and leads to a sense of invulnerability. We are all human, and our decision-making is biased by our own experiences and self-perspectives. A good leader will drive the decision and discussion processes to others so that they can get balanced input and feedback.

9. *Have high expectations.* Hold other people accountable for achievement and set a good example for them to follow. Encourage continuous improvement within your organization and provide ongoing change within your organization so that people will be comfortable with change and adapting the organization to new environmental opportunities.

10. *Cultivate a wide perspective* both on the environment, the organization and your clients and industry. You are not going to see every change which may emerge, but if you are constantly scanning the environment and having strategic dialogs with others outside your own industry you will have the opportunity to see the shifts and changes more clearly.
11. Finally, it is said that the best leaders are the ones that *you don't see*. They are constantly working behind the scenes to empower and grow their subordinates, allowing them to continue to grow their own skills. They don't know jealousy—their world is organized around the success of others and they know that their rewards will come with the success of others.

I hope you have enjoyed this book. It is difficult to pack a larger perspective of the capitalistic perspective, organizational strategy, and professional development and leadership skills into a single book. Hopefully I have been successful in providing a primer for pulling all of these together and synthesizing these concepts. My ultimate goal was to give the young (and not so young) professional a map of the road ahead, and to let them know what skills and values to begin to start developing. I'd be glad to get your feedback on what I've missed and what should be added in the future.

SELECTED ADDITIONAL READING

If you have found that these concepts have been enlightening to you and you would like to learn more about them, the following section provides additional reading by chapter. These are the books that I have personally used and recommend in my own personal journey toward leadership.

Table of Contents
1. Acknowledgments
2. Introduction of the Processes

Overview
3. Person, Profession and Adding Value
4. Person & the Organization
5. Person & Perception
6. Personal "Brand"
7. The Environment
8. Professional Stages
9. Leadership Skills

Technical Skills
10. Welcome to the Working World
11. Depth vs. Breadth
12. Helping others & Building Relationships
13. Leadership Skills

Professional Skills
14. Project Management
    A Guide to the Project Management Body of Knowledge, 4th Edition, Project Management Institute, ANSI/PMI 99-001-2008
15. Client Focus
16. Team Focus
17. Work Motivation and Drive
18. Emotional Intelligence
    Working with Emotional Intelligence, Daniel Goleman, 1998, Bantam Books.
19. Leadership Attributes
    WICS: A model of Leadership in Organizations, Sternberg (2003), Academy of Management Learning and Education, Vol. 2, No. 4, 386-401.

Management Skills
20. Understanding the Organization
    The Personal MBA, Josh Kaufman, 2012, Worldly Wisdom Ventures LLC
21. Adding Value.
22. Leveraging Value
    An Organizational Learning Framework: From Intuition to Institution, Crossan, Lane & White,

Academy of Management Review, 1999, Vol. 24, No. 3, 522-537.
23. Management vs. Leadership Skills
Managers and Leaders: Are they Different? Abraham Zaleznik, 1992, Harvard Business Review, Mar-Apr 1992.

Leadership Skills
24. Critical Thinking & Decision Making
The Psychology of Decision Making. Lee Roy Beach, 1997, Sage Publications
25. Shifting Skills
26. Social Intelligence
Social Intelligence, Daniel Goleman, 2006, Bandam Books
Primal Leadership, Goleman, Boyatzis & McKee, 2013, Harvard Business Press
27. Role of Executive Coach
Coaching for Leadership, Goldsmith, Lyons & Freas Eds, 2000, Jossey-Bass/Pfeiffer
28. Leadership Processes
Leadership in Organizations (Chapter 9), Deanne N. Den Hartog & Paul L. Koopman, Handbook of Industrial, Work and Organizational

Psychology, Vol. 2. *Managing Creative People: Strategies and Tactics for Innovation,* Michael D. Mumford, Human Resource Management Review, 2000, Vol. 10, No. 3, 313-351.

ABOUT THE AUTHOR

Charles L. "Chip" Pickering graduated from West Virginia Wesleyan College with a BS in Engineering Physics and Minor in Mathematics. He obtained an MS in Engineering Management from Marshall University's College of Graduate Studies and a Ph D in Strategic Leadership from Ohio University.

Chip has been involved in the construction industry since 1980 and established an engineering company, Pickering Associates, in 1988. Since then Pickering Associates has developed into a regional Architectural-Engineering-Surveying company. Chip recently founded a renewable energy company, Pickering Energy Solutions.

Chip is a Professional Engineer and Fellow with the National Society of Professional Engineers, is an Advanced Practitioner with the US Green Building Council (LEED) for Building Design and Construction, is a NABCEP Certified Photovoltaic Installation Professional and has a Project Management Professional certification from the Project Management Institute.

Chip has taught business, management and leadership classes at the university level as well as LEED, PMP and other certification and training courses. Chip frequently lectures on leadership, green energy and sustainable construction. Chip has always been interested in Leadership training, and has mentored and coached many young professions on career development.

Chip lives in Williamstown, WV with his wife, Jan, and travels to Africa to support ongoing renewable energy projects in Liberia. Their short-term goal is to finish their section hike of the Appalachian Trail.

Additional information on Chip's activities and projects can be found on our website www.cpickering.us and through related links. Chip can be reached at clp@cpickering.us.

[i] Wikipedia, Profession, retrieved 1-13-14.
[ii] For additional information on developing more rational perspectives there are several good websites such as www.criticalthinking.org which has a more detailed process for beginning to be more reflective about your thinking processes.
[iii] Mayer, J.D., Salovey, P., Caruso, D.L., & Sitarenios, G. (2001). Emotional intelligence as a standard intelligence. Emotion, 1, 232-242.
[iv] Goleman, D. (1998). Working with emotional intelligence. New York: Bantam Books

CITATIONS

www.ingramcontent.com/pod-product-compliance
Lightning Source LLC
Chambersburg PA
CBHW020857180526
45163CB00007B/2534